Little Kid Crafts For All Seasons

Kid Tested Crafts That Parents Love Too!

By Chris Yates

TruSite Inc. In cooperation with

KidCraftsMagazine.com
FreeKidCrafts.com

Copyright © 2012 by Chris Yates and TruSite Inc.

All Rights Reserved.

Templates and craft instruction pages may be reproduced for individual sue or classroom use only, not for commercial resale. No portion of this publication may be reproduced for storage in a retrieval system, or transmitted in any form or by any means, electronic, mechanical, recording, etc., without the written permission of the publisher. Reproduction of these materials for an entire school, school system, or day care is strictly prohibited. Reproduction of these materials on websites, blogs, and newsletters is strictly prohibited.

Little Kids series is written, illustrated, and edited by Chris Yates and TruSite Inc.

TruSite Inc.
2028 S. Hwy 53, Ste 3, PMB 326
La Grange, KY 40031

NOTICE: The information contained in this book is true, complete, and accurate to the best of our knowledge. All recommendations and suggestions are made without any guarantees on the part of the author or publisher. The author and publisher disclaim all liability incurred in conjunction with the use of this information and encourage adult supervision of young children at all times.

Dedicated to my children Katie, Jack, and Sidney.
They are the inspiration for everything I do.

Contents

Contents 5
Forward 9
A Few Notes Before We Start… 13
   How This Book Is Organized 14
   A Few Ground Rules… 15
   Preparation Is Golden… 16
A Note On Safety… 18
Recycling 19
   Special Art Frame 20
   Crazy Toilet Paper Tube People 22
   Easy Paper Tree 24
   Under Water Ocean Scene 26
   Toilet Paper Tube Monkey 28
   Soda Bottle Snowman 31
   Fall Toilet Paper Tube Tree 34
   Long Tube Snake 36
   Toilet Paper Tube Frog 37
   Milk Jug Bird Feeder 42
Paper Plates 45
   Family Flower Garden 46
   Paper Plate Monsters 48
   Paper Plate Fish 50
   Paper Plate Clown 52
   Mary's Tired Lamb 54
   Silly Summer Hat 56
   Funny Flat Frog 58
   What Makes A Rainbow? 61
   Spring Spiral Garden Mobile 64
Template Crafts 69
   Corner Cat 69
   Paper Car Puppets 73
   Caterpillar Pin 77
   Turtle Plant Poke 80

My Color Book	83
Easy Butterfly Napkin Ring	87
Fish Scales	93
Scarecrow Stick Puppet	97
Spring Bird's Nest	101
My Winter Counting Book	104
Simple Ladybug Windsock	107
Beach Day Photo Frame	114

Hand Print Crafts ... 119

Hand Print Stegosaurus	120
Handprint Peacock	122
Handprint Air Freshener	124
"Handy" Elephant	126
Handprint Lion	128
Hand Print Hermit Crab	130

Paper Bag Crafts ... 133

Paper Bag Bee	134
Fall Gathering Basket	136
Paper Bag Elephant	138
Paper Bag Mittens	140
Lion Paper Bag Puppet	142

Exploration and Learning Crafts ... 149

Leaf Creatures	150
Clay Letters	152
Name Necklace	154
Print Making	156
Flower Blow Painting	158
Winter Toothbrush Painting	160
Egg Head People	162
Ink Blot Kites	164

Holidays ... 167

Quick n' Easy Gift Wrap	167
Handprint Key Chains	170
Hiding In A Pencil Holder	172
Warm Fuzzy	175
Valentine Dangle Heart	178

- **Pot of Gold** 180
- **Pine Cone Easter Bunny** 182
- **Handprint Easter Chick** 184
- **Show Your Patriotism** 186
- **Traditional Candle Centerpiece** 189
- **Egg Carton Christmas Tree** 192
- **Shrinky Dink Ornament** 194
- **Toilet Paper Tube Turkey** 196
- **Paper Plate Witch** 203
- **Q-Tip Skeleton** 206
- **Clothespin Bat** 208
- **Christmas Scape** 212

Forward

Writing this book has been a very personal experience for me. I began this book and my own website out of sheer disappointment in what was available to parents, preschool teachers, daycare workers, and other people who work with small children. After searching through every online resource I could find and buying just about every book ever written on crafting with younger children, I walked away with the feeling that this area of kids' crafts has been severely overlooked. Most of what I found was either too old for my kids, the same or reworked projects on free sites, or completely commercialized.

Sure, you can find a wealth of books on crafting with school age children. In fact, some of the books for this age group are absolutely beautiful and have original content, but let me ask you:

How many books or other resources do you find for Little Kids?

I don't mean elementary school kids, I mean toddlers and preschoolers. You'll find many books that claim to be for children ages 2 or 3 to 6, but I can tell you from my own experience that they are really aimed at the 5 and 6 year olds. I've bought many of these books only to be disappointed to find that they had 2 or 3 crafts, out of 50 or more, that were projects that my 3 year old could do.

In fairness, crafting with toddlers and preschoolers does come with its own set of challenges. At this age kids have just about no attention span, have to be constantly monitored, often don't have any concept of what they are supposed to be making, and are only capable of very simple tasks.

Challenging, but not impossible...

Most craft books that claim to be for toddlers and preschoolers have crafts that require an adult to do so much project assembly that it becomes more an adult project than a child's project. Don't get me wrong, some adult assistance is necessary for any craft project or activity that you do with Little Kids, but some of the crafts that I've seen and tried to do with my own children were so difficult or time consuming that my children lost interest within minutes.

Looking back, it's kind of funny to think that I'm trying to "help" them put their project together while they are entertaining themselves by finger painting my kitchen walls, the table, and themselves.

The second thing that really irritated me about Little Kid crafting is the lack of originality. I can't tell you how many books that I have purchased that had only a handful of original ideas, while the bulk of the book was dedicated to super-sized pictures and rehashed material available in 20 other books. In other words, they had very little substance.

There is a series of children's crafting books out on the market today (I don't think it would be right to name it.) that dedicates two pages to each craft idea or project. On first glance, this may not seem like a lot, (most of my projects take two pages too) but here's a reality check:

More than half of each of the two pages is taken up by unnecessary pictures - pictures that don't add to the value of the craft or its description.

After purchasing several books in the series, I discovered that many of the crafts were just about identical. Here's some examples:

In one book there is a project that does apple prints with paint. The next book in the series does vegetable prints.

In the same book there is a "Recycling Sculpture" using blocks of Styrofoam and later there is a "Wood Sculpture" using scrap pieces of wood. Then of course there are other "original" projects like an oatmeal container drum, woven berry baskets, cardboard box buildings, a king's crown, and the infamous clothespin butterfly.

If all this regurgitated garbage weren't enough, many of the rest of the projects are far too old for little hands. For example: shred crayons with a potato peeler onto a piece of paper, fold it over and put an iron on it to melt the crayons.

Now, what part of this project do you want your 2 or 3 year old to do? Should they handle the sharp potato peeler or the hot iron?

Believe it or not, I bought several books similar to the one described above for $12.95 each - What a waste of money!

Then I started my online search for more crafting inspiration with my own children. I've looked at hundreds of websites over the course of the last few years. Most of them have three things in common:

- They are full of banner ads, pop-ups, and false recommendations for products that are either unrelated to kid crafting or products that the site owners have obviously never used themselves.

- They contain only a handful of the same old projects you've seen a thousand times interspersed among the advertisements.

- They are so poorly organized and difficult to browse or search that you can't find anything.

These are the things that prompted me to build my own websites dedicated to crafting with kids. You've probably already visited it if you're reading this book. It's at:

www.FreeKidCrafts.com
www.KidCraftsMagazine.com

My sites have very little advertising on them, and anything that is advertised on the sites are for products that I have used, or my children have used. I have used a lot of software and technology on the website to make it easy to browse the crafts and to search for particular craft ideas. Lastly, I continuously add new crafts and activities to the sites... and not just the same ideas you see all over the internet. I'm proud of the sites and I think I've done it right. They are the kind of websites that I would like to visit.

And so now in this second edition, after selling thousands of copies in simple ebook format, I'm finally able to offer <u>Little Kid Crafts For All Seasons</u> in a bound book (physical edition) as well as a Kindle edition.
The craft ideas in this book are not available on my site and they aren't in any of my other books. These are my own original ideas specifically written for this book - and I've got pages of handwritten notes to prove it!

It is my sincerest wish that you find it a useful part of your kid crafting library and that it shines as an example of how children's crafting books should be written.

Best Wishes and Happy Little Kid Crafting!

Chris Yates

A Few Notes Before We Start...

Crafting with Little Kids can be tremendous fun for you and your child when you pick age-appropriate activities, prepare all the materials in advance, and dedicate your time to that crafting period. Crafting can be frustrating, maddening, and a total pain in the neck if you don't.

When it comes to crafting with Little Kids, it is less important that the craft looks like what it's supposed to and more important that it provides a good, creative outlet for the child.

Who cares if the cow's tail is coming out of his nose and the sun is green?

Give your child the freedom to do it his or her way. That's the most important gift you can give your child when you craft with them.

Whenever possible, I like to make crafting with my kids part of a bigger picture. Crafting is just one of the things built into our daily and weekly routine.

- We do phonics and letter work.
- We play on the piano.
- We do skill building worksheets.
- We do a little foreign language study.

All this in addition to free play, role play, sports, special trips, etc. The kids and I do a lot together and crafting plays a big role.

I try to develop crafts each week that all fit into a theme. For example, if we're planning a zoo trip, we'll do crafts for the week before, and sometimes the week after, that revolve around a zoo theme. You already know how this works from my website, so I won't explain it again here.
The crafts in this book don't follow any particular theme. They represent a wide range of crafts that could each be used as part of several different themes.

How This Book Is Organized

The projects in this book are organized into different sections according to the kind of crafts they are – recycling, paper bag, holidays, etc.
You'll find hand print crafts, paper plate crafts, template crafts, holiday crafts, recycling crafts, memory crafts, and learning crafts… Something for everyone!
In addition, I've given you more ideas on how to use each of the crafts.

- If the craft is too difficult for your child, I've given you ideas on how to make it a little easier.

- If your child's skill level is beyond the craft, then I also give you ideas to make it more challenging.

- I even give you ideas on how to adapt each craft to use it for other themes, or along with other ideas.

In other words, there are many more craft ideas within this volume than first meet the eye. This book will provide a jumping off spot to go on to create your own ideas and craft projects.

If that isn't enough, I also outline some ways you can use each craft as a skill builder or use other learning tools to get double duty out of each craft. I tried to write each of the crafts out in such a way that you could get the absolute most out of each and every one.

A Few Ground Rules...

Alright, "ground rules" probably isn't the right way to say it, but here are a few things you need to know about my instructions in this book.
I often talk about stapling different components together instead of gluing them. There are a couple of reasons for this:

1. First of all, stapling is so fast. If you are helping a young child put a project together, they are going to quickly lose interest if you are gluing pieces together and have to wait for them to dry before continuing with the project. Stapling a project together is quick and allows them to immediately admire and play with their creation. If it's a part of the project that a parent has to help assemble, thin I'll probably recommend stapling. If it's something that a child can do unassisted, then use the glue.

2. Occasionally, I call for hot glue. This is also a parent-only job. I only call for hot glue on parts of a project that require parental assistance. If you are working with a little older child that can assemble everything themselves, then let them use white glue or a glue stick instead.

3. Speaking of glue sticks, I'm a big fan of them. When I'm crafting with my own children, we use glue sticks whenever possible. They are less likely to wrinkle or discolor paper, and they are a lot less messy than ordinary white household glue.

4. When I refer to craft sticks, this is what I mean:

   Large Craft Stick = Tongue Depressor
   Small Craft Stick = Popsicle Stick

5. When I refer to a paper plate, I generally mean a cheap 9 inch paper plate that doesn't have any wax coating on it. These are the kind of paper plates that you get a couple of hundred plates for a couple of bucks. I will specifically state that a heavy duty plate or a smaller plate is necessary if that's what's required for the project.

Preparation Is Golden...

Preparing your materials and your craft in advance is probably the most important factor in whether the craft time with your child is fun for you both or whether it is full of stress for you and leads to tears and frustration for your child.

Here are a few things to thing about.

1. **If Possible, do the draft for yourself the night before you plan to do it with your child.**

    This serves two purposes. First of all, it gives you the opportunity to see what parts of the project may be difficult for your child to do, so you may want to change something in the project.

    Sometimes you will find that a particular idea just won't work with your child and you have to scrap it. Better to find out before you try to sit down with your child and do it.

2. **Gather all your materials before you sit down to craft.**

    This is a hugely important factor in a successful craft session with your child. If you have to keep popping up to get some supply needed for your project, you're probably going to come back to a disaster.

Children have such short attention spans anyway, so if you make them wait while you go and get the next supply, they will either give up on the project entirely, or find something else to entertain themselves, like cutting their bangs or sprinkling glitter all over the floor.

Having everything assembled in advance, including covering your surface with newspaper, gathering smocks and protective clothing, and preparing cleanup materials like soap and water will make the entire craft project a stress free, fun, and memorable time for you and your child.

A Note On Safety...

I'm sure you are a very safety minded adult and you don't need me to give you a long song and dance about how to keep your kids safe during crafting. Having said that, I still want to mention a few things.

1. Don't walk away and leave a child unattended while crafting. There's all kinds of things that could happen to hurt them, not to mention destroying the craft area.

2. Don't let kids do parent jobs like stapling, hole punching, using hot glue, etc.

3. If you're using small objects like brads and buttons, don't let your child put them in their mouth. Small objects pose a choking hazard and should be monitored.

4. Only let children use child safety scissors to cut.

5. Only use non-toxic paints, crayons, markers, glue, etc.

6. Closely monitor kids around any object that is hot like a hot glue gun or oven. Little Kid skin burns easily.

Recycling

Special Art Frame

This is a really fun and simple "picture frame" that you can do for just about any picture your child creates. Although it's not a frame in the traditional sense, it will still make any picture appear more special and makes a great gift that kids can make themselves.

You'll Need:

- Construction Paper
- Clean Styrofoam Meat Tray
- Crayons or Markers
- Glue
- Yarn or Ribbon
- Sharp Object to Make Holes

Directions:

1. Have your child draw or color a special picture of their family or something else that is special to them onto heavy construction paper.

Make sure it will fit inside the meat tray first.

2. Glue the picture to the center of a Styrofoam meat tray. Let the glue dry.

3. Use a sharp object like a nail or ice pick to make 2 holes in the top of the meat tray.

4. Thread a piece of yarn through the holes and tie the ends together to make a hanger for your framed artwork.

NOTE: The size of the piece of paper the child should color depends on the size of the Styrofoam meat tray that you use in this project. Try to use a piece of paper that's about 3-4 inches shorter in length and width than your meat tray.

More Ideas...

- Meat trays come in all different colors. You could use a colored meat tray to create a different looking frame for your artwork.

- Glue tissue paper, beans, buttons, or pasta around the edge of the frame for a more decorated look.

- To make this project more challenging, use a plastic needle and yarn to sew all around the outside edge of the frame.

- Create a simulated glass front for your frame by covering it with plastic wrap or cellophane.

- Use a dull point to make dents in the Styrofoam and create even more unique designs for your frame.

Craft Tip...

You may want to try to use a glue stick to glue the artwork to the frame so it doesn't wrinkle. Otherwise, just put glue in the corners instead of spreading it over the entire tray to reduce wrinkling.

Crazy Toilet Paper Tube People

This is one of those projects that you can go back to again and again because kids have so much fun making them. Over the years we've made everything from monsters to Santa Claus using this same basic project idea.

You'll Need:

- Clean Toilet Paper Tube
- Construction Paper
- Tissue Paper
- Scissors
- Clue
- Crayons, Markers, Stickers, etc.

Directions:

1. Cut a piece of construction paper into a 4.5 x 6 inch rectangle. Use it to cover a toilet paper tube. Glue in place.

2. Draw different people parts onto construction paper and cut them out. You can cut out eyes, nose, lips, ears, earrings, ties, eyebrows, glasses, or whatever else you want.

3. Glue the people parts onto your tube to make a funny looking tube person.

4. Cut tissue paper into 4 - 5 inch squares. Put several of the squares over the top of a pencil and insert into the end of each tube. Remove the pencil and you should have "hair" sticking up from the heads of your tube people.

NOTE: Don't forget to name your people!

More Ideas...

- You can make different tube people for different occasions... Teachers, mail carriers, mad scientist, Christmas, Independence Day, etc.

- You don't have to cut out body parts for your tube person, you can just as easily draw them with a marker or crayons. This might be a little easier for younger children.

- You can color your tube people with any color of construction paper that you want... They don't have to be "people colors."

- Cut pictures of different features out of magazines and glue them to your tubes instead of drawing them.

Craft Tip...

A glue stick works well for this project instead of white craft glue because of the drying time.

Easy Paper Tree

This is such a simple idea, yet it makes a big impact with the kids when it's done. It's also a great way to get in some practice with scissors… even the child with the worst coordination can still make a beautiful tree!

You'll Need:

- Clean Toilet Paper Tube
- Brown Construction Paper
- Green Construction Paper
- Scissors
- Glue

Directions:

1. Cover the toilet paper tube with a 4.5 x 6 inch piece of brown construction paper. Glue in place.

2. Roll 2 sheets of green construction paper into a tube, lengthwise, and insert it into the toilet paper tube. Push is through until it is even with the bottom of the tube, and let go.

3. Cut slits in the green paper tube about half an inch apart all the way around the tube. You should make your cuts all the way down to where the toilet paper tube starts.

4. After all the cuts are made, gently pull up on the green paper to make the tree branches appear. (Do not pull the paper all the way out of the toilet paper tube.)

Skill Building: This project is a great opportunity for kids to get in some scissor practice. Even less coordinated children can make most of the cuts

Craft Tip...

When you roll the green paper up into a tube, start your roll with just 1 sheet of paper, then add the second one part way through the rolling. It will give the tree more depth after it's cut and pulled out.

More Ideas...

- Use fall colored paper instead of green to make a fall tree.

- Glue small paper bugs, butterflies, or flowers to the end of the "branches" to make a much more elaborate tree.

- This project would be great for a tropical or jungle theme since it looks a lot like a palm.

Under Water Ocean Scene

This is one of those projects that can be as simple or as elaborate as you want to make it. I once did this one with a small group of kids, some of which were as old as eleven and as young as three, and they each created a masterpiece that they could be proud of.

You'll Need:

- Green Construction Paper
- Scraps Construction Paper
- Clean Styrofoam Meat Tray
- Sand
- Blue Marker
- Crayons
- Scissors
- Glue
- Cellophane or Plastic Wrap

Directions:

1. Draw a line across the inside of a Styrofoam meat tray that is 2 - 3 inches from the edge. This is the sea bottom line. Color the inside of the tray, above the line, with a blue marker. It doesn't matter if it's completely covered.

2. Cut fish shapes out of different colors of construction paper. Randomly glue them to the bottom of the meat tray, in the blue part.

3. Tear pieces of green construction paper into long skinny pieces to resemble sea weed and other sea plants. Glue them to the tray so that the bottom of each plant in either even with the line or a little below.

4. Spread glue across the meat tray on the empty side of the line you drew in step 1. Sprinkle sand on the glue. Try to cover that 2 - 3 inches of tray completely with sand so the ocean floor will look real. The line of sand should be a little bit ragged rather than a perfect line. Let glue try completely.

5. After glue is completely dry, gently shake the excess sand off the tray. Cover the entire tray with clear cellophane, pulling it taught. Make sure you use a big enough piece to overlap in the back of the tray.

More Ideas...

- Instead of coloring the tray blue with a marker, complete the scene and then cover with blue colored cellophane.

- Glue small shells to your sea floor.

- Draw coral on construction paper, cut out, and glue to your ocean floor after you glue the sand on. You can also add different creature to your scene like crabs, lobsters, eels, sharks, and whales.

- Cut out small circles of light blue paper to make bubbles.

- You could use a Styrofoam meat tray that is already blue to really make this project go fast.

- Experiment with different sizes of trays, or turn them different directions.

Toilet Paper Tube Monkey

This little monkey is just plain fun and it's super easy to do with the template that I've provided.

If you don't have any clean toilet paper tubes, you can substitute paper towel rolls cut in half, or make your own tube out of an old file folder. Simply cut the size you want and staple it on one side to make a tube.

You'll Need:

- Clean Toilet Paper Tube
- Brown Construction Paper
- White Construction Paper
- A Printer or Copy Machine
- Scissors
- Glue
- Crayons

Directions:

1. Print the template at the end of this section out on white construction paper. Color the monkey with crayons. Cut out the pieces.

2. Cover the toilet paper tube with a 4.5 x 6 inch piece of brown construction paper, and glue in place.

3. Glue the monkey's knees onto the tube according to the diagram below. Glue his upper body onto the front of the tube, on the opposite side of where his knees are glued. Glue his feet onto the bottom of the tube.

More Ideas…

- If you want to make this craft more challenging, print out the upper body and the knees on brown construction paper. Then print out the smaller body parts (face, feet, and ears) on white or tan paper.

- Color as appropriate and cut out. Glue the light body parts over top of the brown ones and assemble the monkey.

Craft Tip…

Be sure to print out your template before you begin this craft. It will be frustrating for children to have to wait while you print it.

Toilet Paper Tube Monkey Template

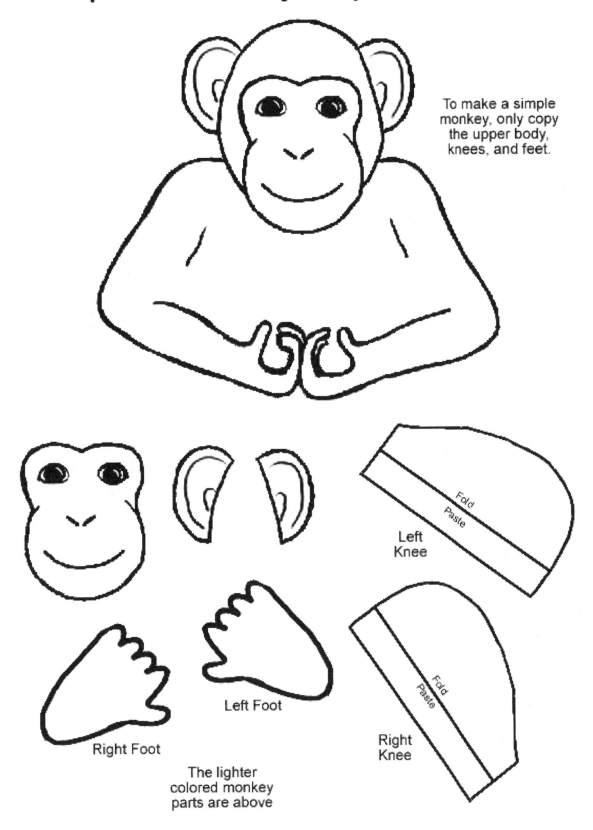

To make a simple monkey, only copy the upper body, knees, and feet.

Left Knee

Right Knee

Right Foot

Left Foot

The lighter colored monkey parts are above

© KidCraftsMagazine.com

Soda Bottle Snowman

What a great project to do in the wintertime when it's too cold to go outside and play!

Young children will enjoy this craft because it really looks like something when it's done, but older kids will enjoy it too because they can make it look like a "big kid" project.

You'll Need:

- 20 oz. Soda Bottle
- 1 Man's Tube Sock
- 1 Colored Woman's Sock
- ¼ C. Sand (Optional)
- Scrap Black and Brown Construction Paper
- 1 Large Pom Pom
- Red Felt
- Glue
- Scissors

Directions:

1. Pour 1/4 Cup of sand into a clean soda bottle and put the lid on. This step is optional, but will weigh snowman down so that he doesn't fall over.

2. Put bottle inside a man's tube sock and push it all the way down to the toe of the sock.

The neck of the bottle should be at the open end of the sock. Tie a big knot in the open end of the sock. This is the snowman's body. (The knot will be covered by the hat.)

3. Fold up the cuff of the colored sock and put it over the top of the snowman's body to make a hat. The hat should cover the knot and the top curve of the bottle so it will stay on by itself.

4. Tie a piece of red felt around the bottle to make a scarf.

5. Cut circles of black paper for the eyes, nose, mouth, and buttons. Glue in place. Cut 2 "stick" arms from brown paper. Fold back the end of the arms about a quarter of an inch to make a tab. Glue the tab onto the snowman to make the arms.

6. Glue a large pom pom to the top of the hat.

More Ideas...

The things you could do with this project are really endless, especially since it has such an easy base to start with. Here are a few of the things you could try:

- Use wiggle eyes or pieces of felt for the face.

- Make an orange cone of paper and glue on for a carrot nose.

- Make a scarf out of yarn or a strip of material and try embellishing the snowman with lace, ribbons, paper, feathers, buttons, stickers, cut outs, etc.

- If you want to make the snowman really easy, simply draw on all the facial features with a black permanent marker.

Fall Toilet Paper Tube Tree

I really like any project that uses the child's hands or hand prints. I especially like this one because it helps children to think creatively when they have to consider the idea that their fingers become the branches on the tree.

You'll Need:

- Brown Construction Paper
- Scraps of Fall Colored Paper
- Clean Toilet Paper Tube
- Scissors
- Glue
- Pencil

Directions:

1. Wrap a 4.5 x 6 inch piece of brown construction paper around a toilet paper tube and glue in place. This will be the tree trunk.

2. Trace around your child's hand onto brown construction paper. Cut out and glue onto the side of the tube towards the top and opposite the seam. This will be the tree's branches. (See the illustration at right.)

3. Tear pieces of fall colored paper into pieces and glue onto the "branches" to make the leaves.

More Ideas...

- Try this project with pastel colored paper for a spring tree.

- Use fall colored tissue paper for a completely different look.

- This is a good opportunity to talk with your child about the seasons, as well as how and why the leaves change. You might even take them out to collect leaves of their own.

Craft Tip...

Glue sticks work well for this craft. They dry quickly, keep things moving, and are a lot less messy.

Comments...

This a great Autumn keepsake craft!
Don't forget to write the date on the back.

Long Tube Snake

This is an especially fun craft for the youngest crafters to do because it lets them practice their coordination.

It also makes a fun toy when they're done!

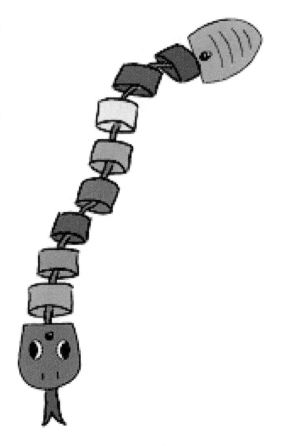

You'll Need:

- 4 Toilet Paper Tubes or 2 Paper Towel Rolls
- Printer and Paper
- Markers
- 24 Inches of String or Yarn
- Thin Cardboard
- Scissors
- Glue Stick

Directions:

1. Cut each of the 4 tubes in half. Color each of them different colors with markers.

2. Print out the head, tail, and tongue or trace them onto paper. Glue each of the parts to thin cardboard. Color with markers.

3. When glue is dry, cut out the pieces. Punch a hole in the top of the head and the base of the tail as indicated. Glue the tongue to the underside of the head so it sticks out.

4. Assemble the snake: Thread one end of the yarn through the hole in the tail and tie off. String the colored tubes onto the string - the tail should keep them from coming off. Tie the head on through the hole you punched to complete the snake.

More Ideas…

- To make this craft easier for younger children, you can cut down on the number of tubes used.

- To make it more difficult, paint the tubes or color patterns on each of the tubes.

- You can also use construction paper rolled up into tubes instead of toilet paper tubes, but it won't hold up as well to a child's handling.

Toilet Paper Tube Frog

I am absolutely crazy about frogs, and this is a fun project for the kids to make a frog that stands up on its own.

This is a great project for spring, or anytime you're working in a water, jungle, or zoo theme!

You'll Need:

- Clean Toilet Paper Tube
- Printer and Paper
- Green Construction Paper
- Glue Stick
- Scissors

Directions:

1. Print the template on the next page out on green construction paper. Cut out the pieces.

2. Cover the toilet paper tube with a 4.5 x 6 inch piece of green construction paper, and glue in place.

3. Glue the eyes onto the frog's body. Glue the frog's knees onto the tube according to the diagram below. Glue his feet onto the bottom of the tube. Glue his upper body onto the front of the tube, on the opposite side of where his knees are glued.

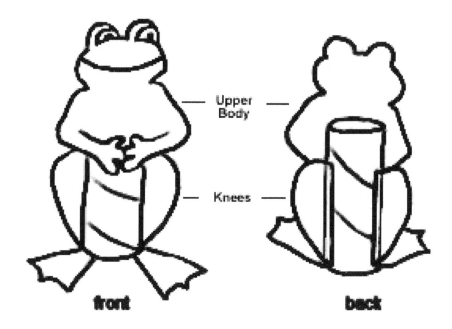

Craft Tip...

Be sure to prepare your template before you begin this craft. In addition, you may want to cut out the eyes in advance.

You can print and color the template with crayons as an alternative to printing it on green construction paper.

Note...

They eyes on the template are there in case you want to print on white paper and color the template. Use the eyes to the left and print on white paper if you're printing the body on green paper.

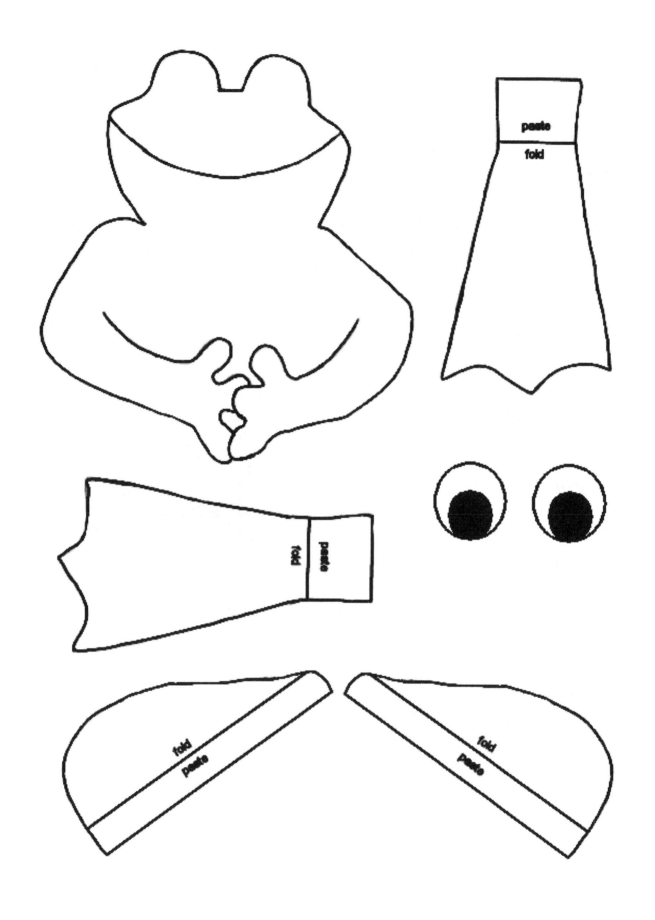

KidCraftsMagazine.com 41

Milk Jug Bird Feeder

Although an adult will need to prepare the basic bird feeder before the kids are turned loose on it, the kids will still have a blast painting it... And they'll be so proud of their project when it's done!

You'll Need:

- Empty Gallon Milk Jug
- Sharp Knife (for adults only)
- Acrylic Paints
- Paintbrush
- 4 Popsicle Sticks
- Twine or String

Directions:

1. Using a sharp knife, cut out sections of the milk jug on all four sides. Sections can be as large or small as you want, but should be about 2 inches from the bottom. See diagram below.

2. Cut a small slit underneath each open section of the milk jug. This is where you'll insert the popsicle sticks to make perches. Also poke a hole through the threaded neck of the milk jug on opposite sides. This is where you'll thread through a piece of twine to hang your bird house.

3. Use the acrylic paint to paint the outside of your bird house. Let dry completely.

4. Insert the popsicle sticks into the slits about half way. Thread a piece of string or twine through the 2 holes in the neck of the milk jug. Fill with the bird seed of your choice and hang it up outside.

Skill Building...

Most young children have already noticed the birds around them, but this project gives you a good opportunity to talk to them about birds in more detail. For example, you can talk about what kind of birds you have in your area, what they eat, migration, etc.

You can also go on a nature walk with your child and do a little bird watching.

Craft Tip...

Use a knife that's been heated up with a lighter - it makes the plastic cut like butter and I think it makes the raw edges of plastic a little less sharp. However, only do this with a knife that won't conduct the heat to the handle, be sure to keep the hot knife away from the kids, and make sure the plastic is completely cooled before starting to paint.

Paper Plates

Family Flower Garden

Kids love looking at pictures of themselves, their family, and their friends, so what better way to celebrate those relationships than creating a cute little flower garden... It's very easy to make and the kids will enjoy looking at it when it's done!

You'll Need:

- 1 Large Paper Plate
- Tempera Paint
- Pictures You Can Cut
- Glue
- Paintbrush
- Scissors
- Green Construction Paper

Directions:

1. Copy or find a picture of each family member and cut it into a circle measuring 4 - 5 inches.

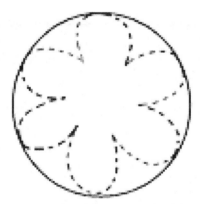

2. Paint the back side of a paper plate the color of a flower... any flowery color will do. Let dry.

3. Cut plate to resemble a flower with petals. Make sure you leave at least a 5 inch center.

4. Glue a picture of a family member to the center of each flower.

5. Cut a stem and leaves out of green construction paper. Glue on to flower.

6. Do this for each family member, then tape your flowers to a wall or door to create a family flower garden.

More Ideas...

- This is a really cute idea to put up in a child's room. It's much safer than putting up pictures in frames and is a cheery addition.

- This would be a great gift for a child to give to a younger sibling or in preparation of a new birth.

- Preschools or daycare providers could use this idea for their classroom bulletin board and put up a picture of each "flower child."

- A child could create a "Friend Flower Garden" or even a "Pet Flower Garden."

- Flowers come in all different shapes and sizes. You could make each of your flowers the same or you could have tulips, sunflowers, etc.

- You could easily use other ideas to decorate your basic flower, such as coloring with markers, using stickers, covering with tissue paper, using torn scraps of colored paper, etc

Paper Plate Monsters

This looks like a very complicated project, but it's simpler than you think, plus it makes a great looking monster when complete, whether you go for the scary kind of Halloween monster or the fun, silly kind of monster.

You'll Need:

- 2 - 9 Inch Paper Plates
- Tempera Paint (Any Color)
- Markers
- Construction Paper
- Glue
- Scissors
- Paint Brush
- Any Other Supplies You Want to Use to Make Your Monster Interesting and Fun

Directions:

1. Paint the back side of both paper plates any color you want. Let dry completely.

2. Draw on a face with markers. Be sure to add interesting features to your face such as glasses, eyebrows, moles, etc.

3. Cut several strips of paper that are about 5 - 6 inches long and 2 inches wide. Gather together 4 or 5 strips of different colors and sandwich them between the 2 plates. Staple together. Do this all the way around the head of your monster. (And beard if you want.)

4. Cut slices into the strips of paper, creating fringe all around the plate. Use your hands to bend and crinkle the fringe. The messier it looks the better.

NOTE: Very young children will not be coordinated enough to do the assembly of the monster, but they'll be able to do the rest easily.

More Ideas...

- Paint your plate any wild color you can think of to make it more fun.

- Make glasses out of pipe cleaners and glue them on your face.

- Cut a hat out of construction paper and glue it onto your paper plate.

- Make a bow out of ribbon and glue it into the hair of your paper plate monster.

- Add a collar or bow tie made from construction paper to make your monster look like it sits on a body.

- Cut the eyes out of your plate and glue it to a large craft stick to make it a silly monster mask.

- Staple 2 paper plates together, right sides together, with a space around the bottom left open. Slip your hand in to make a puppet.

Paper Plate Fish

This is one of my very favorite paper plate projects because it's so simple to do and the kids love it. The best part is when they talk about how the little fish is about to get eaten... Their faces just light up.

You'll Need:

- 9 Inch Paper Plate
- Tempera Paint (Any Color)
- Paint Brush
- Black Marker
- Construction Paper
- Hole Punch
- Fishing Line
- Glue
- Scissors
- Tape

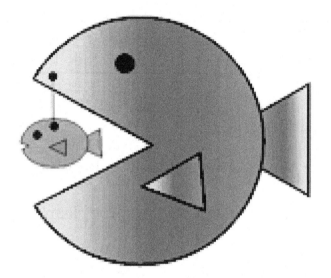

Directions:

1. Paint the back side of a paper plate with any color tempera paint. Let dry completely.

2. Cut a triangle out of the paper plate that resembles a pie slice. This will be the fish's mouth.

3. Cut the tip of the triangle off about 2 inches down. This will be the tail of the fish. Staple it to the paper plate on the side opposite the cut out for the mouth.

4. Use the tip of the triangle to make the fin of the fish. Glue it in place. Draw an eye on your fish with a black marker.

5. Double over a piece of construction paper and cut out a second fish that is about 3 inches long. This will give you two identical fish. Draw an eye in the same spot on both little fish.

6. Cut a piece of fishing line that's about 4 - 6 inches long. Tape one end of the fishing line to the back of one of the little fish. Glue the other little fish on top of the other one to sandwich the fishing line in between. Tape the other end of the fishing line to the back of the paper plate fish so that it hangs down inside the opening of his mouth.

Skill Building...

- You could take this opportunity to talk to your child about how bigger fish eat little fish, what fish eat, etc.

- This is a good project for an ocean or a fish theme week.

More Ideas...

Instead of painting the fish, assemble it as directed, then draw on scales with markers and color the fish.

Paper Plate Clown

This is another one of those projects that can be as elaborate or as simple as you choose to make it, based on the age of your child. Even older children would enjoy this project, which is something to keep in mind if you have several children of varying ages.

You'll Need:

- Any Color Construction Paper
- 9 Inch Paper Plate
- Markers
- Scissors
- Large Red Pom Pom
- Any Other Color Large Pom Pom
- Stapler

Directions:

1. Draw a clown's face in the middle of the back side of your paper plate with markers. Glue a large red pom pom on for a nose.

2. Glue pieces of yarn all around the top edge of the plate to make hair.

3. Cut a half circle that measures about 10 inches across out of construction paper. Decorate the hat with polka dots, stickers, etc. Fold the outer edges near the flat side together to form a cone. Staple in place.

4. Staple the bottom edge of the hat onto the clown's head. You will have to staple it over some of the hair. If you need to flatten the hat out a little to staple it in place, that's alright.

5. Cut a long strip of paper that's about 2 inches wide and as long as your paper. Accordian fold the strip. This will be the collar. Staple each end of the strip to the plate where the collar should be and then staple in a couple of times in the middle, between the folds.

6. To finish the clown, glue a pom pom to the point of the hat.

More Ideas...

- You can experiment with other kinds of hats for your clown. They wear all different kinds of hats.

- Put pom poms around the edge of the hat and glue them on the hat to act as polka dots.

- You can use other kinds of material for the hair such as raffia, cotton balls, paper, etc. or you can omit the hair all together.

- An old cone-type party hat would make a cute clown hat. Simply cut off the elastic cord and staple in place.

Craft Tip...

You can try to glue everything for this project instead of stapling, but using a stapler is much quicker and easier, especially since an adult will do the stapling.

Mary's Tired Lamb

I think this is the cutest project... but maybe that's because I have a soft spot for lambs. Although the assembly of this craft might need to be done by an adult if your child is very young, they'll still enjoy gluing on the cotton balls. And they'll love the finished project!

You'll Need:

- 2 Large Paper Plates
- 1 Small Paper Plate
- Black Construction Paper
- Cotton Balls
- Glue
- Black Marker
- Stapler

Directions:

1. Cut 4 squares, 5 inches each, of black paper. Roll each square into a tube measuring 1-2 inches across. Staple in place.

2. Lay a large paper plate, right side up, on a flat surface. Lay the second one on top of the first, right side down. Staple them together once to hold them in place.

3. Flatten down one end of a tube and staple the flat end between the 2 plates. You'll do this 3 more times to create the legs.

The legs should stick out from the paper plates about 3-4 inches. See the picture below for leg placement on the lamb. This is the lamb's legs and body.

4. Cut two floppy ears out of black construction paper. Staple them to the small paper plate. Draw a face on the small paper plate with a black marker. This is the lamb's head.

5. Staple the bottom of the head (the chin) to the front of the body.

6. Glue cotton balls all over the lamb's body and head, sparing the legs, face, and ears.

More Ideas...

- Glue a bow onto the lamb's head to make this a girl lamb.

- To simplify this project, use just one plate. Cut out black legs and glue on the bottom of the plate. Draw a face towards the outer edge of the plate between the two front legs, and then cover with cotton. The lamb is much more one dimensional this way, but the real fun for kids is gluing all the cotton balls on the plate.

Craft Tip...

The lamb's head will sit up more or less, depending on how thick the cotton balls are behind the head.

Silly Summer Hat

This is a really fun, basic project that you can do no matter what time of the year it is. Although this one is made for summer, you could do one for a holiday, a sport, a special occasion, a particular theme you're working with, a trip to the zoo, etc. The possibilities are endless!

You'll Need

- 2 Large Paper Plates
- Stapler
- Watercolor Paint
- Paint Brush
- 24 Inches of Ribbon or Yarn Things to Decorate: yarn, ribbon, foam shapes, pom poms, paper, glitter, feathers, buttons, etc.
- Scissors
- Glue

Directions

1. Paint the back side of one paper plate and the front and back side of the other with any color of watercolor paint. Let dry. You can also choose to leave the plates uncolored, especially if you have a lot of stuff to decorate them with.

2. Put the plates together with painted sides touching. Staple 2 times in the center of the plates.

3. Cut 2 pieces of ribbon 12 inches long. Staple one piece of ribbon on either side of the plate that's only painted on one side. Staple the other piece of ribbon on the opposite side of the same plate.

4. From this point on, you can decorate the hat any way you want.

More Ideas...

- You can really use any kind of materials to embellish this hat, including the suggestions in the supply list.

- You could paint the plates with acrylic or tempera paint instead of watercolors to make a much brighter hat.

- You could make this project much quicker and easier for younger children by putting the hat together and then turning them loose with crayons and markers, instead of paint. This way you wouldn't have any drying time before you could decorate the hats.

- These hats make great kid party activities.

- Create the same basic hats, but then decorate them for a specific theme, such as Valentine's Day or St. Patrick's Day.

- Staple a paper bowl and a plate together instead of two plates to make a different kind of hat.

Funny Flat Frog

Yes... I know, it's another frog, but can you really have to many frogs? This frog project is about as simple as you can possibly get, and the kids will love his tongue!

You'll Need

- Paper Plate
- Green, Red, Black, and White Construction Paper
- Green Tempera Paint
- Paint Brush
- Scissors
- Black Marker
- Glue

Directions

1. Paint front side of a paper plate with green tempera paint. Let dry.

2. Cut 2 frog arms and 2 frog legs from green construction paper, using the template on the next page.

3. Cut 2 large eyes out of scrap white paper. Cut 2 pupils out of black paper.

4. Cut a long strip of red paper that is about an inch wide and 10 inches long (depending on how long you want the frog's tongue to be._

5. Glue the arms and legs to the unpainted side of the paper plate. Check out the picture on the previous page for placement.

6. Glue the pupils to the white eyes, and glue the eyes to the top side of your frog (the painted side).

7. Glue the tongue to the unpainted side of the plate where the mouth would be. Wrap the tongue around a pencil tightly and then release it to make it curl upward.

8. Draw on nose holes and a mouth line with a black marker.

More Ideas...

- Don't limit yourself to just making green frogs. Frogs come in just about every color of the rainbow.

- Some frogs also have spots and stripes on them. You can put some on your frog with paint or by drawing them with a marker.

- Try coloring your paper plate with markers, instead of paint, to make the project go a little faster.

- Get some fly stickers to put on the frog's tongue to make it really fun... or if you're talented, draw and cut out the fly yourself.

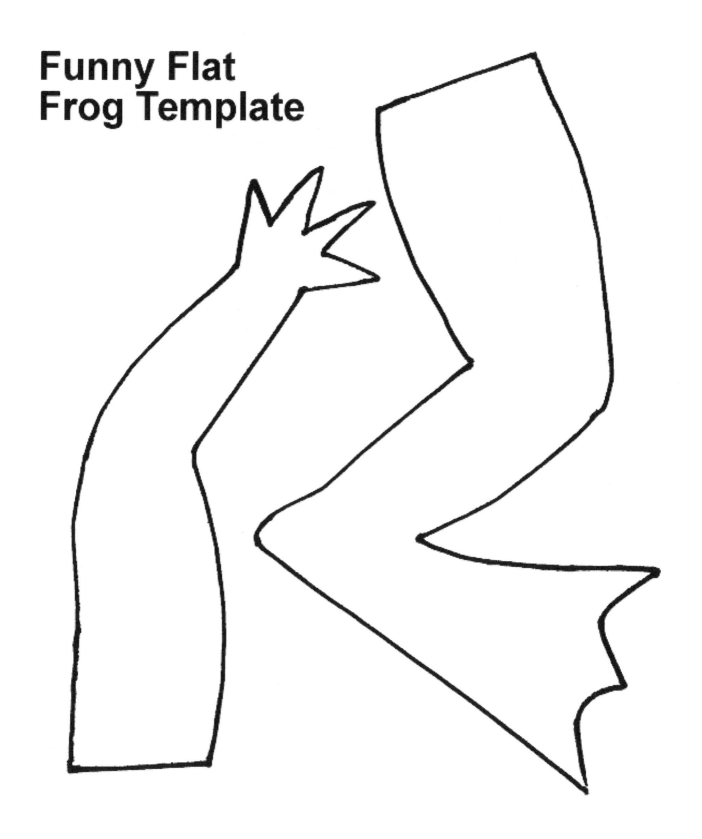

What Makes A Rainbow?

Anytime kids see a rainbow, they always wonder how it's possible and what makes it work. Why not turn this natural curiosity into a craft project?

You'll Need:

- 1 Large Paper Plate
- 2 Small Paper Plates
- Markers
- Scissors
- Hole Punch
- Yarn or String
- Glue or Stapler

Directions:

1. Fold a large paper plate in half and then cut it in half on the fold line. Color one of the plate halves like a rainbow with markers.

2. Cut a small paper plate in half, and then cut the scallops on it to make it look like the top part of an umbrella. Cut a large "J" from the other half of the plate. Staple or glue the "J" onto the umbrella to make a handle. Color with markers.

3. Color a small paper plate with a yellow marker. Older kids can cut triangles out of the edge of the plate to make the sun's rays.

4. Using hole punch, punch a hole in the top of the umbrella and the top of the sun. Punch a hole on each side of the rainbow. Attach a piece of yarn or string from the umbrella to the hole on the left side of the rainbow. Attach a piece of yarn or string from the sun to the hole on the right side of the rainbow.

5. Punch one hole in the top of the rainbow and attach a piece of yarn or string to make a hanger.

Skill Building...

- Talk with your child about what actually makes a rainbow. (The raindrops or moisture refract the sun light as it passes through each tiny drop.)

- The concept of refraction is pretty difficult, so you could use terms like changes, or turns into, etc.

- You can also talk about what colors make up a rainbow. They are listed below from the top of the arc to the bottom in order:

Red
Orange
Yellow
Green
Blue
Indigo
Violet

Spring Spiral Garden Mobile

This is a cute little mobile this really easy for younger kids to put together, plus it makes them feel like I've accomplished something when they finish.

You'll Need:

- Printer and Paper
- Large Paper Plate
- Hole Punch
- Scissors
- Glue Stick
- Markers or Crayons
- String or Yarn
- Mobile Template

Directions:

1. Print the template at the end of this section out on regular computer paper. Color the pictures.

Cut each of the rectangles out on the dotted line, but don't cut the dotted line separating each set of twin images.

Fold each rectangle in half on the dotted line, and glue wrong sides together. This will give you double sided mobile pieces.

2. Cut plate starting at outer edge and spiraling towards the center. Stop cutting when you get about 2 inches from the center.

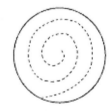

3. Punch a hole in the center of your plate. Thread a piece of string or yarn through the hole and tie a large knot in the end.

The knot should be large enough to keep it from coming back through the hole. Tie a knot in the string on the opposite side of the plate to keep the string from coming out of the hole on the other side.

This is your mobile hanger.

4. Punch one hole in the outside of your plate at the spot where you started your spiral cut. This should be the pointed end of the cut plate.

Punch 5 more holes in your plate, evenly spaced, along the edge of the spiral cut. This is where you'll hang your mobile pieces. Take a look at the diagram on the right for clarification.

5. Punch a hole in each of your mobile pieces and thread a piece of string through the hole. Tie off.

Thread the other end of each of the mobile pieces through the holes in the paper plate and tie off.

More Ideas...

- Glue the mobile parts to thin cardboard, then cut out to make a more sturdy mobile.

- Paint both sides of the paper plate and let dry. Then continue with the project.

- Use fishing line, instead of string or yarn, to make a mobile that seems to float in the air.

- Instead of cutting around the objects on the dotted line and making rectangle objects, older kids could cut around individual objects to make this more challenging.

- Decorate your mobile with glitter, sequins, etc. to make it sparkle.

Comments...

This is one of the easiest mobiles for young children to make because you don't have to worry about balancing out all the pieces.

Template Crafts

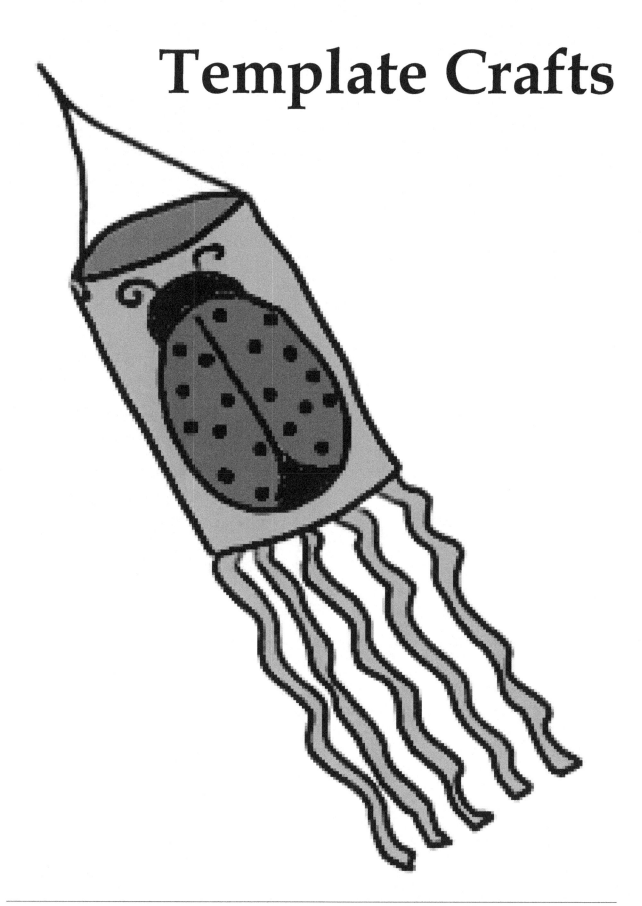

Corner Cat

This is one of my daughter's favorite crafts when she was little because it was something that she could hang up in her room and she was done and admire. If your child's an animal lover there's sure to love this one.

You'll Need:

- Corner Cat Template
- Printer
- Thin Cardboard
- Glue
- Construction Paper
- Scissors
- Crayons or Markers
- Corner Cat Template

Directions:

1. Print out the template on the next page onto heavy white construction paper.

2. Color the cat with crayons or markers. Don't cut out yet.

3. Glue the cat onto thin cardboard. Let the glue dry completely, then cut out.

4. Put your cat up on the corner of a door jam so that it looks like it's sitting on the doorway and about ready to jump off. You may have to loop a piece of tape and place it on the back of the cat to keep it up on the wall.

NOTE: If you're working with kids that are a little bit older this craft works really well using craft from the set of cardboard and paper. It stands up better, but you still may have to put tape on the back to get it to stay up well.

More Ideas...

- Print the template out onto any color of construction you want, then proceed through the project.

- Cover the eyes on the template with wiggle eyes.

- Embellish your cat by tying a piece of ribbon around it's neck to make a collar. You could even put a bell on the ribbon.

- You can create several of these corner cats and place them around your house. Small children will get a big kick out of them.

Craft Tip...

A glue stick works really well for this project because it doesn't wrinkle the paper the way ordinary white glue does.

Corner Cat Template

Paper Car Puppets

Younger children will especially love this craft. When my son was very young, he would spend hours playing with these little cars and rolling them around on top of the couches, the chairs, the countertop, or anything else that he could find.

You'll Need:

- Construction Paper
- Brads
- Large Craft Stick
- Scissors
- Hole Punch
- Black Marker
- Car Puppet Template

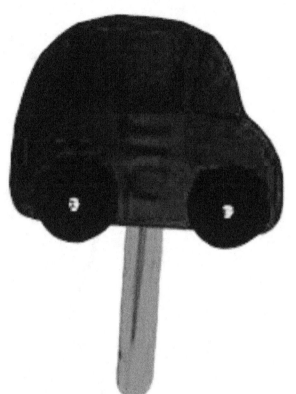

Directions:

1. Draw a car shape on construction paper or use the template at the end of this section. The car should be about 5-7 inches long and about 4 inches tall. Cut out.

2. Cut 2 circles that are approximately 1 1/2 inches in diameter out of black paper. These are the wheels.

3. Punch a hole in the center of each wheel. Measure the wheels against your car and punch holes in your car where you want the center of your wheel to be.

4. Push a brad through the hole in your wheel and then through the corresponding hole in your car. Open the brad up on the back side of the car to secure the brad and the wheel. Do the same with the other wheel.

5. Draw windows, door handles, people, etc. on your car with a marker.

6. Glue a craft stick to the back side of your car. Let the glue dry completely before you try to play with the car.

More Ideas...

Cut all your shapes out of thin cardboard and paint or cover with construction paper for a more durable car puppet. Cereal box cardboard works great. The wheels will turn better on the car if they are made of cardboard as well.

Don't limit yourself to just car puppets. You can make any kind of vehicle: trucks, fire engines, etc. My son even tried to make a trash truck!

Caterpillar Pin

This is a super easy craft kids will love. It goes especially well with several books themes, if you like to tie your crafts into your book reading, and it also makes a nice way to decorate the classroom, a child's room, or simply where the pin on the front the kid's T-shirt.

You'll Need:

- Pom Poms
- 2 Wiggle Eyes
- Scissors
- Glue
- Green Construction Paper
- Pinch Type Clothespin

Directions:

1. Print out or make a copy of the leaf below on green construction paper. Cut it out.

2. Put a line of glue on the line down the center of the leaf. Glue the pom poms to the leaf in a line. Put the pom poms as close together as possible.

3. Glue the 2 wiggle eyes onto the first pom pom in the line to make a head.

4. Glue the leaf onto a clothespin. Put the pointy end of the leaf on the end that you pinch to open the clothespin. Let the glue dry completely.

After glue is dry, the caterpillar can be clipped to clothing, to make a safe caterpillar pin.

Skill Building...

- Very young children can practice their eye hand coordination by putting the pom poms on the line on the leaf.

- Manipulating small pom poms also helps them work on their fine motor skills.

- Cutting the simple outline of the leaf below also gives kids a little cutting practice.

More Ideas...

- To make this pin more durable, cut the leaf out of thin cardboard and paint or color green.

- You could also make the leaf out of felt.

- Make several of these pins and clip them to things all over the house for a fun Spring decoration.

Turtle Plant Poke

I love any craft that actually creates a product that kids can play with or use for some other purpose. This plant poke project fits the bill nicely. Although the craft is designed to be something that you poke into a flower pot to dress up a plant, it can also be used as a puppet.

You'll Need:

- Turtle Template
- Printer
- Green Construction Paper
- Scissors
- Glue
- Large Craft Stick

Directions:

1. Print out the template at the end of this section onto heavy green construction paper.

2. Cut around the square outline, but do not cut on the dotted line.

3. Fold on the dotted line. This is your turtle.

4. Insert a craft stick from the bottom of the turtle up to the fold. Glue the two sides of the turtle together, sandwiching the craft stick in between them. Let the glue dry.

5. Poke the turtle, stick first, into the potting soil around a house plant. Be careful not to hit any of the plant's roots.

> **Note**: Kids are good at cutting can cut around the turtle itself, rather than cutting the square around the turtle. Younger children can practice of cutting skills by just cutting around the turtle on the square.

More Ideas...

- Print the template out onto white construction paper and color all the parts. Then proceed through the project.

- Cover the eyes on the template with wiggle eyes.

- Glue small pieces of green and yellow tissue paper all over the turtle's shell to make it more three dimensional and a little more challenging.

- Use a thin dowel instead of a craft stick if you're working with a little older kids. (Younger kids may poke themselves with it.) A dowel is easier to poke into a plant than a craft stick.

- Create your own template for other kinds of plant pokes. Flowers, animals, or other objects work really well.

Craft Tip...

A glue stick works really well for this project because it doesn't wrinkle the paper the way ordinary white glue does, and the paper will stick well to the craft stick with a glue stick.

KidCraftsMagazine.com

My Color Book

Kids love to make little booklets, and this one is ideal for younger kids who are just beginning to learn their colors.

You'll Need:

- Printer
- Typing or Printer Paper
- Crayons
- Hole Punch
- 18 Inch Piece of Yarn
- Color Book Templates

Directions:

1. Print the 3 templates on the following three pages on plain typing paper.

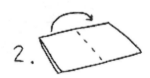

2. Assemble the book according to the diagram.

Fold it in half and then in half again on the dotted lines. Put all the folds together.

The order of the pages really doesn't matter, as long as the cover is on the front of the book.

3. Punch holes where indicated by the circle on the cover page while the book is lined up. Punch hole through all layers.

4. Fill Thread yarn down through the holes from the top, cross on the bottom, and then thread back up through the holes from the bottom. Tie in a bow at the front of the book.

4. Color the pages of the book in order.

Craft Tip...

Wrap a piece of tape around the ends of the yarn to make it easier to thread the yarn through the holes. You can snip off the tape when you're done.

Skill Building...

- Homemade booklets are a great way to reinforce the concept of colors as well as the idea that books read from left to right - a concept difficult for young children to grasp at first.

- Let your child read the book to you to really drive the point home!

yellow sun

red strawberries

This Color
Book Made By:

_____

My Color Book

© KidCraftsMagazine.com

orange

grapes
purple

green frogs

blue bird

pink flower

white snowflake

brown cow

black bat

Easy Butterfly Napkin Ring

This little napkin ring craft is a great way for kids to make something useful for their families. This craft is so cute, that even older kids will want to get in on action and make their own napkin rings.

You'll Need:

- Printer and Paper
- Crayons, Colored Pencils, or Markers
- Scissors
- Napkin Ring Template

Directions:

1. Print out the template at the end of this section. These were printed on plain printer paper, but you can also us cardstock for a sturdier napkin ring.

2. Color the butterfly halves any way you desire. Crayons or colored pencils work best. Cut out each template.

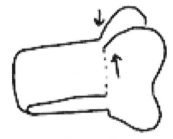

3. Cut on the 2 dotted lines as indicated. Do not cut all the way through. Only cut halfway. Fit the two cuts into each other. See the diagram below for clarification. When the napkin ring is put together correctly, it will look like there is a butterfly fluttering on top of each ring.

More Ideas...

- This is a great way to roll up napkins for a planned picnic. It's also a great way to give kids something to do when you're trying to get ready to have people over for a barbecue or other get together.

- Try printing out the template on colored paper for a very different looking napkin ring.

- You can use glitter on your butterfly to make it something really special.

- For a more durable project, try printing out the template on heavy construction paper or cardstock instead of plain printer paper.

- You could cut antennas from black construction paper to give it an even more 3-D effect.

Craft Tip...

If you have trouble getting your napkin ring to stay together, you can add a small piece of transparent tape to the inside of the ring where the two sides join.

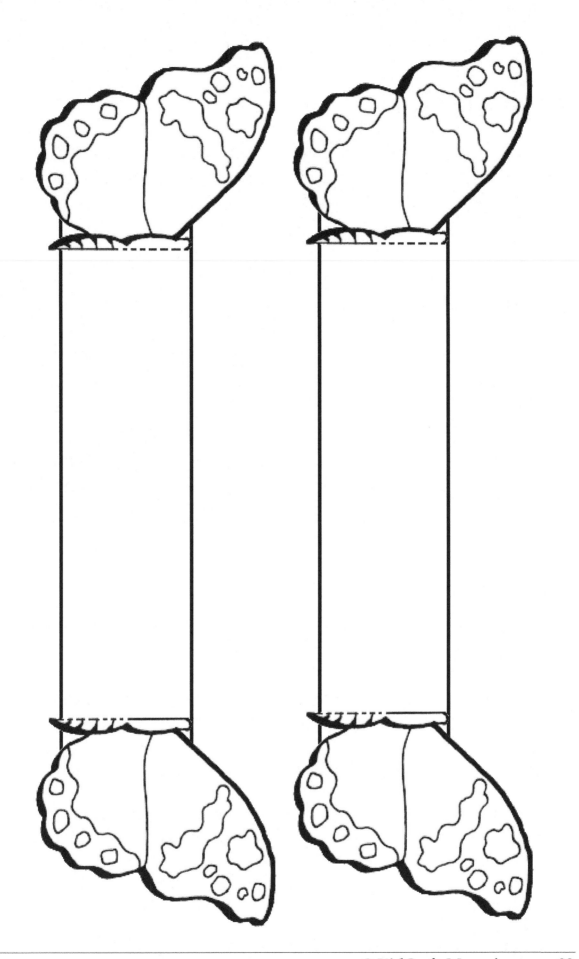

Fish Scales

This is a very simple project, but one that will help children learn to think out of the box. It also gives children the opportunity to paint with their fingers, something that all kids love to do.

You'll Need:

- Sheet Construction Paper
- Tempera Paint
- Small Paper Plate
- Printer
- The Template

Directions:

1. Print out the picture on the next page on any color construction paper.

2. Color as much or as little of the picture as desired with crayons before moving in to the next step. Be sure to leave the fish uncolored, so that you can proceed on with the next step without waiting for paint to dry.

3. Pour a small amount of tempera paint into a small paper plate.

4. Show the child how to dip their finger into the paint and stamp it in a row across the fish to make scales. Let them continue stamping and fill in the fish with scales. Let dry completely.

NOTE: You may have to help your child with putting the first row scales on their fish so that they understand what they're supposed to do, especially if they are very young.

Skill Building...

When doing this craft project, don't forget to talk to your child about what fish scales are, how they protect the fish, etc. You could even make it part of an ocean or fish theme.

More Ideas...

- Try using washable stamp pads instead of tempera paint for the scales. It washes up easier and you can see each individual fingerprint better.

- Do the whole project with fingerpaints on fingerpaint paper. Have child draw the fish in its natural habitat and then put on the scales all with fingerpaint.

Comments...

This is a fun project for children and an easy one for adults. Kids love putting their hands in paint and stamping on paper, and adults love projects with little preparation that kids can do themselves.

Scarecrow Stick Puppet

Little kids will love making this simple puppet project, especially since the puppet's arms and legs move. This is a great and simple project for Fall, Halloween, or even Thanksgiving.

You'll Need:

- Scarecrow Template
- Printer
- Heavy Printer Paper or Construction Paper
- Scissors
- 4 Brads
- Large Craft Stick
- Markers or crayons

Directions:

1. Print the template at the end of this section on heavy paper or construction paper.

2. Color the scarecrow's parts and cut out.

3. Glue the hat onto the head. Glue the hands onto the arms. Glue the feet onto the legs.

4. Attach the legs to the body with brads at the "x". Do the same with the arms. You can use the picture on the previous page as reference for attaching the arms and legs.

5. Glue a large craft stick to the back of the scarecrow so that it can be used as a handle for the puppet. The brads will allow the scarecrow to be posable.

More Ideas...

- Glue the scarecrow's parts to thin cardboard, color and cut out. Using cardboard will make the puppet much more durable.

- Glue paper between the head and the hat and cut it into fringe to make it look like straw. You can do the same between the hands and arms and between the feet and legs.

- Instead of using paper to make straw, you could glue small pieces of raffia onto the puppet.

Comments...

Very young children will have trouble cutting out all the pieces, but they will enjoy coloring the scarecrow and playing with him when he's put together.

Spring Bird's Nest

This is a super simple project for younger kids to do completely on their own. This craft can also be tied into a lot of different learning themes in a preschool classroom setting such as studying birds, animal themes, eggs themes, etc. It's also nice because you can turn this into recycling project by collecting things in the environment.

You'll Need:

- Sheet Blue Construction Paper
- Brown Construction Paper
- Other Scraps Construction Paper
- Scissors
- Glue
- Miscellaneous pieces of straw, sticks, yarn, etc. for nest

Directions:

1. Cut a nest shape out of brown construction paper. Cut out a couple of bird or egg shapes from the appropriate color of construction paper. This will depend on what you want in your nest.

2. Draw a line of glue on the construction paper. Have child glue all the things that go in a nest on the line.

3. Glue the nest on top of the eggs and birds so that they look like they are sticking out of the nest.

4. Glue pieces of straw, small sticks, yarn, cotton, etc. onto the nest. When done, the paper nest will actually resemble a real nest. Let glue dry before handling.

Skill Building...

- Talk with your child about how birds build nests to lay their eggs in to keep them safe.

- Explain that birds will build their nests out of whatever materials they find available: straw, twigs, grass, hair, etc.

- I've even seen nests built using pieces of tinsel and Easter grass.

My Winter Counting Book

This counting book is a great way for kids to do a little crafting a little coloring and practice their numbers at the same time. Once they've completed the counting book, you can continue to work with them and refer to the book as they learn their numbers.

That makes this craft fun for the kids and useful at the same time. I love that!

You'll Need:

- Counting Book Templates
- Printer
- Typing or Printer Paper
- Crayons
- Hole Punch
- 18 Inch Piece of Yarn

Directions:

1. Print the 3 templates on the following three pages on plain typing paper.

2. Assemble the book according to the diagram. Fold it in half and then in half again on the dotted lines. Put all the folds together.

Make sure numbers are in the right order.

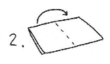

3. Punch holes where indicated by the circle on the cover page while the book is lined up. Punch hole through all layers.

Thread yarn down through the holes from the top, cross on the bottom, and then thread back up through the holes from the bottom. Tie in a bow at the front of the book.

4. Color the pages of the book in order.

Skill Building...

Counting books are a great way to reinforce the concept of numbers. They have a good opportunity to associate the number with the number of objects on each page as they are coloring their book. In addition, after the project is complete children will continue to "read" their counting book over and over again.

Craft Tip...

Wrap a piece of tape around the ends of the yarn to make it easier to thread the yarn through the holes. You can snip off the tape when you're done.

Comments...

This little book will feel like a real book to kids because the pages are doubled up. It will read like a real book because it's double-sided. Don't forget to brag on your little author when they are done - better yet, sit down and let your child read it to you!

10

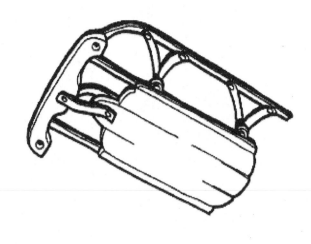

1

This Winter Counting Book Made By:

_____

© KidCraftsMagazine.com

My Winter Counting Book

9

5

7

4

Simple Ladybug Windsock

Windsocks are a fun craft for kids to make at just about any age, but especially very young children. What makes this one even more fun is having a great template to work off of.

You'll Need:

- Windsock Template
- Printer
- Heavy Construction Paper
- Glue
- Stapler
- Scissors
- Yarn or String
- Hole Punch
- Crayons
- Streamers

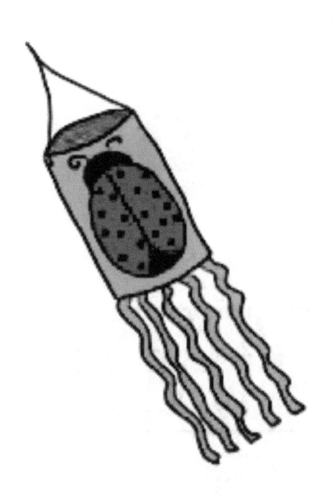

Directions:

1. Print out the template at the end of this section on heavy white construction paper. Color the ladybugs.

2. Cut several streamers that are 12 - 18 inches long.

3. Turn the ladybug template face down on a flat surface. Place a strip of glue across the long end of the template, opposite the ladybug's heads. Glue the end of your streamers to the bottom of the template. Let dry.

You can also staple the streamers in place if you don't want to wait for the glue to dry.

4. Roll the paper up into a cylinder and overlap up to the dotted line. Staple in place.

5. Punch 2 holes near the top of the cylinder where indicated. Thread yarn through holes and tie off to make a hanger for your windsock.

> **NOTE:** This windsock can't be put outside in the weather. It's best hung near a window where it can catch a breeze in the house.

More Ideas...

- Use a heavy piece of green construction paper to make the cylinder. Print the ladybug template on red paper and cut out. Color in all the black parts with a black marker and complete the project with green streamers.

- You could also make the cylinder out of thin cardboard, paint it, and then glue on the red ladybugs.

Craft Tip...

Tape over the yarn and the hole on the inside of the windsock, after you've threaded it through and tied it off. This will help keep the yarn from pulling through the construction paper.

You could also use paper hole reinforcers on the inside of the windsock.

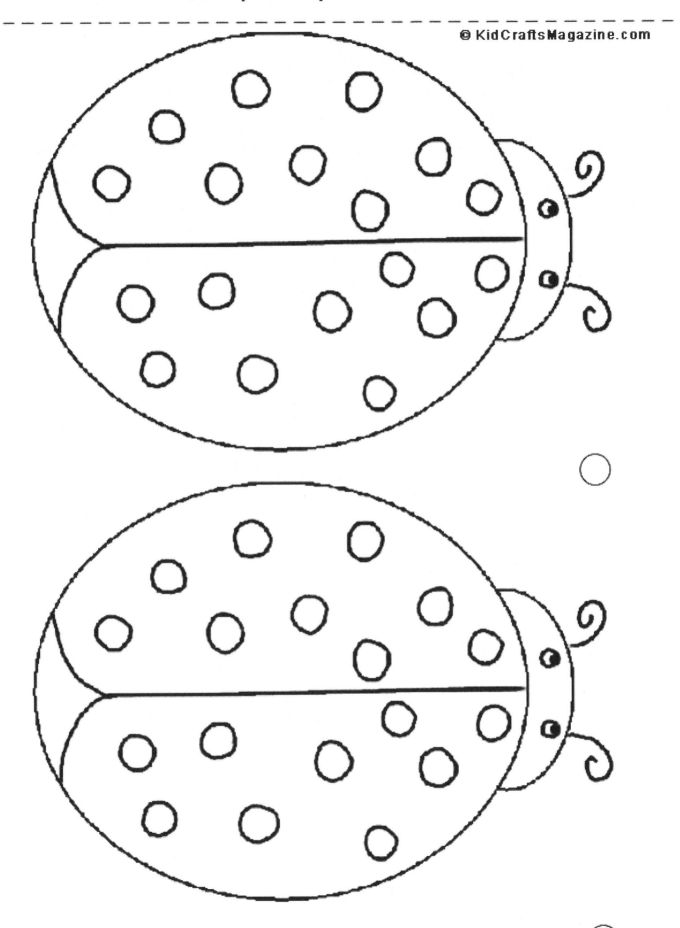

Beach Day Photo Frame

Picture frame crafts a great project to do for both kids and their parents. They make great keepsakes and they're a lot of fun for kids of all ages to make

You'll Need:

- Frame Template
- A Printer
- Printer Paper
- Thin Cardboard
- Scissors
- Glue
- Markers or Crayons
- Transparent Tape
- 4 x 6 inch photograph

Directions:

1. Print out the template at the end of this section on printer paper or construction paper.

2. Color the frame.

3. Glue the frame to thin cardboard and let dry. Cut out picture frame, including the center hole.

4. Fit the frame over your photo and tape it to the frame on the back side.

More Ideas...

- Glue a loop of ribbon to the back to make a hanger.

- Use archival tape instead of scotch tape so that picture and frame can be placed in child's scrapbook.

- Cover photograph with contact paper or put a thin piece of plastic between frame and photo to protect it.

- Write the title and date or year to create a keepsake.

Craft Tip...

- Glue sticks work well for this project because they won't soak through the paper or discolor the picture.

- An exacto knife makes quick work of the center hole, but obviously this is for grownups only!

- If you want to use markers instead of crayons, glue the frame onto the cardboard first, then color and cut out.

Comments...

I titled this frame "Beach Day," but that doesn't mean that you can't use it for a photo of a really fun day at the pool or even running through the sprinkler in the back yard.

Hand Print Crafts

Hand Print Stegosaurus

The Stegosaurus is my all-time favorite dinosaur, so I absolutely had to include it in the crafts for this book. Kids especially enjoy drawing the spiky tail and the plates on his back.

You'll Need:

- Construction Paper
- Pen or Pencil
- Markers

Directions:

1. Trace the child's hand onto construction paper with a pen or pencil. Draw a line at the wrist so the handprint to enclose the tracing and make a complete hand.

2. Turn the tracing so that the wrist side is facing up. Draw a spiked tail on the pinky.

3. Draw triangles across the top edge of the handprint from the spiked tail to the middle of the thumb.

4. Draw an eye, nose hole, and a mouth on your stegosaurus.

5. Color it any way you desire.

> **NOTE:** I love this project because it is so simple. My kids are totally fascinated with tracing their hands, and I bet a lot of kids out there do the same thing. They even do it with their crayons on the back of coloring pages and worksheets.

Skill Building...

- You child can practice getting in a little small motor practice by tracing around their own hand.

- This project is a good exercise in "thinking out of the box."

- Talk with your child about dinosaurs, and especially the stegosaurus. Introduce them to a new word: herbivore.

More Ideas...

- Stamp the child's hand with paint, wait for it to dry, then draw the dinosaur around the handprint.

- Trace around the child's hand on colored construction paper, draw the tail and plates across the top, and then cut it out.

- Cut out the handprint and cut out several small triangles. Glue the triangles onto the handprint to create the stegosaurus.

Handprint Peacock

I really love this project because I think it turns out so pretty when it's finished. It's also really simple for kids to make on their own.

You'll Need:

- White Construction Paper
- Green Tempera Paint
- Yellow Tempera Paint
- Blue Tempera Paint
- Paint Brush
- Black Marker
- 3 Small Paper Plates

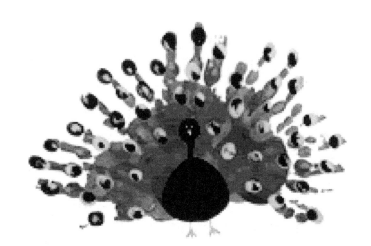

Directions:

1. Pour green tempera paint into a paper plate or pie tin. Dip child's hands into paint and stamp on paper, with fingers spread apart, in a half circle in the middle of the paper. Re-dip the child's hand as necessary. This will be the peacock's feathers.

2. Wash hands. Pour yellow tempera paint into a small paper plate. Have child dip one finger into the paint and stamp fingerprints on top of the handprints. These will be the "eyes" on the peacock's feathers.

3. Pour blue tempera paint into a small paper plate. Have child dip a smaller finger into the paint and stamp on top of the yellow dots.

4. With a paint brush, paint a blue body in the middle of the peacock feathers. The shape of the body should be kind of like a dumbbell, only the bottom end is larger to make the body and the top is smaller to make the head. Let dry.

5. Use a marker to draw in the eyes, beak, and any other details you desire.

Skill Building...

- When doing this project, it would be great if you could bring in a peacock feather for the class to look at. If you don't have one, you may be able to get a "donation" by writing a nice letter to your local zoo.

- This project would be great for a bird theme. Don't forget to talk about the strange noise they make. (It sounds like Help! Help!)

More Ideas...

- Instead of painting the body, you could let the paint dry and cut a body out of blue construction paper to glue on instead.

- You could make this peacock by tracing the child's hand onto construction paper and cutting out several copies instead of painting.

Handprint Air Freshener

This may seem like a strange craft for younger children, but I think it's nice when you can make a craft that's actually useful too.

Younger children will definitely need a little help with this project, but children who are a little bit older should be able to do it themselves.

You'll Need:

- Felt
- Thin Cardboard
- Permanent Marker
- Glue
- Scissors
- Ribbon
- Scraps of Felt, Yarn, Lace, Etc.

Directions:

1. Trace child's hand onto thin cardboard and cut out. This will be your template.

2. Fold a piece of felt in half. Trace your hand template onto the felt with a permanent marker. Cut the hand out, being sure to cut through both layers.

3. Cut a piece of ribbon about 6 - 8 inches long. Glue it to the wrist of one of the felt hands. Glue the second hand onto the first, sandwiching the ribbon ends between the 2 hands.

4. Use scraps of felt, ribbons, lace, yarn, buttons, etc. to embellish your hand. You can make finger nails, rings, bracelets, etc. (You'll be surprised with the ideas kids will come up with for decorating their hands.) Glue the pieces onto the felt and let dry.

5. Put a couple of drops of your favorite essential oil on the felt hand. Hang your air freshener wherever you think things need to smell a little better!

More Ideas...

- This is a great gift idea because it combines a craft with something really useful. In addition, it's really nice to be able to choose your own fragrance.

- This also makes a great gift for Christmas or Mother's Day!

Craft Tip...

- Instead of using ribbon to hang your air freshener, try using elastic string. It comes in a lot of different widths and will allow you to hang your air freshener just about anywhere because it will stretch.

- You can use a lot of different materials to embellish your craft, but paper products don't really work well. They will fade and the oil will leave spots on the paper.

"Handy" Elephant

Although I'm a sucker for just about any handprint craft, I really love this one! It's super simple, kids can do it themselves, and it looks great when it's done.

You'll Need:

- Construction Paper
- Pen or Pencil
- Markers

Directions:

1. Trace the child's hand onto construction paper with a pen or pencil. Draw a line at the wrist so the handprint to enclose the tracing and make a complete hand.

2. Turn the tracing so that the wrist side is facing up. The thumb will be the elephant's trunk and the fingers will be his legs.

3. Draw an ear, tail, eye, and mouth on your elephant.

4. Color your elephant any way you desire.

> **NOTE:** This is a very simple project, but you can make it more challenging by adding a background and creating an entire elephant or jungle theme. You can even add more elephants.

Skill Building...

- You child can practice getting in a little small motor practice by tracing around their own hand.

- This project is a good exercise in "thinking out of the box."

- Talk with your child about elephants, where they live, what they eat, other interesting facts about elephants, etc.

- This is a good project if you're planning a zoo trip, working on a jungle theme, or working on animal theme.

More Ideas...

- Stamp the child's hand with paint, wait for it to dry, then draw the outline of the elephant around the handprint. Finish by drawing in its features with a marker.

- Trace around the child's hand on colored construction paper and cut out. Cut construction paper ears and a tail to make a three dimensional elephant.

Handprint Lion

This is one of my daughter's favorite craft projects. Not only does she love making all the handprints (Is kind of like finger painting.), but she also loves the way it really looks like a lion when she's finished.

You'll Need:

- White Construction Paper
- Brown Tempera Paint
- Orange Tempera Paint
- Yellow Tempera Paint
- 3 Small Paper Plates
- Paint Brush
- Black Marker

Directions:

1. Pour brown tempera paint into a paper plate or pie tin. Dip child's hands into paint and stamp on paper, with fingers spread apart, in a circle in the middle of the paper. Re-dip the child's hand as necessary.

Don't bother to wash hands.

2. Pour orange tempera paint into a small paper plate. Repeat the step above with the orange paint on top of the brown. This will create the lion's mane. Wash hands.

3. Pour yellow tempera paint into a small paper plate. Use a paint brush to paint the lion's head in the middle of the mane. You may have to let the paint dry if you can't get any paint coverage. Don't forget to paint his ears. Let paint dry.

4. Use a black marker to draw in the lion's features -- mouth, nose, eyes, whiskers, etc.

Skill Building...

- This is another great project to do if you are planning a trip to the zoo, working on a jungle theme, or working on animal theme.

- This is a good opportunity to talk a little about lions. You might point out that only male lions have manes.

More Ideas...

- Instead of painting the head onto the mane, you could let the paint dry and cut a head out of yellow construction paper to glue on instead.

- You could make this lion by tracing the child's hand onto construction paper and cutting out several copies instead of painting. You would then have to use a construction paper head or a paper plate to put it together.

Hand Print Hermit Crab

The kids and I took a trip to the mall one day, and came across a vendor who was selling hermit crabs and brightly colored shells. Although we didn't buy any of the hermit crabs, despite the children begging, it was a great inspiration for this craft.

You'll Need:

- Large Pasta Shell (the stuffed pasta kind of shells)
- Red Construction Paper
- Glue
- Markers
- Scissors
- 2 Wiggle Eyes

Directions:

1. Color the pasta shell with markers. The color of the shell really isn't important.

2. Trace the child's hand onto red construction paper and cut out.

3. Put the wrist side of the hand into the open part of the shell as far as it will go and glue in place. This is the crab.

4. Glue 2 wiggle eyes on to the crab. Let glue dry.

Hermit Crab Factoids

- Hermit crabs only have one pincher and they use it to protect their shell when they're hiding inside.

- Hermit crabs shed their skin just like a snake when they outgrow it, as well as taking over a new shell when their home gets too small for them.

- Hermit crabs can regenerate broken or missing legs, claws, or even eyes.

More Ideas...

- You could take this project a step further by putting the crab in a natural habitat. Glue the crab onto a paper plate. Spread glue on the plate all around the crab. Sprinkle with sand.

- This is a good opportunity to teach your child a little bit about hermit crabs. For example you could talk about why they have shells, what happens when they outgrow their home, how they are different than other kinds of crabs, etc.

- You could take your child to a pet store and see what a real pet hermit crab looks like.

- This is an easy project to do with a group of kids for a preschool, daycare, or camp, but you may have to help cut out the hands.

Paper Bag Crafts

Paper Bag Bee

You won't believe how easy it is to make this cute paper bag be. It fits nicely into a lot of different themes, it's simple for kids to do on their own, and it looks really great when it's finished.

You'll Need:

- 1 Paper Lunch Bag
- Yellow Tempera Paint
- Black Tempera Paint
- Black Construction Paper
- Newspaper
- Wax Paper
- Paint Brush
- Scissors
- Glue

Directions:

1. Fill paper bag 2/3 full of crumpled paper. Twist the end of the paper bag into a point. This will be the bee's body and the twisted end will be the stinger.

2. Paint the bee yellow. Let dry.

3. Paint on the black stripes and stinger. Leave the face yellow so you can see the face. Let dry.

4. Draw a face on the bee with black magic marker.

5. Cut 2 antennae out of black construction paper. They should be about 3 1/2 inches long. Fold back a half inch at the end of each antenna to make a tab. Glue the tabs onto the bee.

6. Cut 2 bee's wings from wax paper. They should be about 5 inches long and 3 inches wide at their widest point. Glue them on to the back of the bee as shown below.

More Ideas...

- You can paint the bee yellow, let dry, and then draw the black stripes on with a black marker instead of painting. This may be easier for younger children.

- Use wiggle eyes instead of drawing on the eyes.

Craft Tip...

- When you fill the bag 2/3 full with newspaper, pack it down to make a firmer bee. It will be easier to paint that way.

- Creating tabs for your antennae will allow them to stand up on the bee's head.

- You may have to wrap the bee's stinger with transparent tape to keep it from unraveling.

Fall Gathering Basket

If you're planning to take the kids out to collect fall leaves or other natural objects for another project, this is a great craft to do ahead of time. When they finish with this project, they'll have a pretty little basket, that they've made themselves, to carry their collection in… Plus it so easy to make!

You'll Need:

- Large Paper Grocery Bag
- Scissors
- Stapler
- Fall Decorations: stamps, markers, crayons, stickers, etc.

Directions:

1. Cut the top half of a large paper grocery bag off. Fold over the raw edge about 1-2 inches. This is the bottom part of the basket.

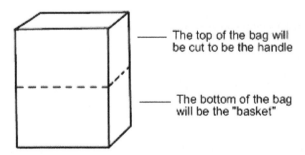

2. Use the top part of the paper bag to make the handle by cutting a strip of the bag that is about 4 inches wide and as long as you want your handle to be. Fold the strip in half, lengthwise, to make the strap a double thickness of paper bag.

3. Staple one end of the handle to the short side of the basket. The end of the handle should be on the inside of the basket. Do the same with the other end of the handle. Staple each end of the handle a couple of times for strength.

4. Decorate your basket with fall stamps, crayons, markers, stickers, etc.

Skill Building...

Now that you've made Fall Gathering Baskets, it's time to do some gathering. Take your child out on a nature walk.

Talk about the changing seasons and what happens in Autumn. Help them to gather leaves, pine cones, acorns, nuts, seed pods, dried vines, etc. This is a good lesson in observation and discovery.

Craft Tip...

Don't paint the basket. Painting the basket might weaken it and make it too fragile to use for a fall nature gathering.

Paper Bag Elephant

Although this project can be a little bit time-consuming because of the time needed to allow the paint to dry, it turns out really cute when it's finished. Kids will really like it because it actually looks like an elephant when it's complete.

You'll Need:

- 1 Paper Lunch Bag
- Elephant Ears Template Below
- Gray Tempera Paint
- Gray Construction Paper
- Newspaper
- 4 Pinch-Type Clothespins
- Scissors
- Glue
- Paint Brush
- Black Marker
- Scrap of Yarn

Directions:

1. Fill paper bag 2/3 full of crumpled paper. Twist the end of the paper bag into a point. This will be the elephant's body and the twisted end will be the trunk.

2. Clip 4 clothespins to the body of the elephant to make the legs.

3. Paint the elephant gray, including his legs. Let dry.

4. Fold a gray piece of construction paper in half and cut out the ear shape for your elephant, using the template below. (Folding the paper in half will give you 2 identical ears.)

Fold the tabs back and glue the ears onto either side of the head.

5. Use a black marker to draw on the elephant's eyes and mouth. Use a scrap of yarn to make a tail and glue that on to your elephant.

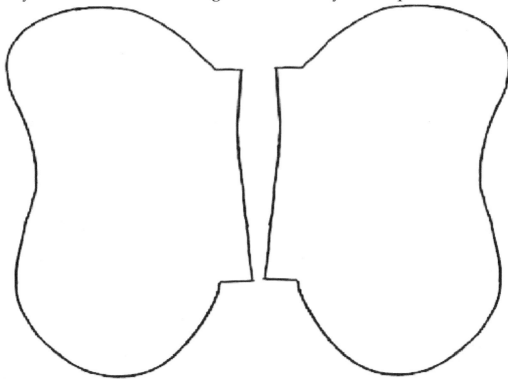

More Ideas...

- You can use large wiggle eyes instead of drawing them on with a marker.

- You can cut a piece of gray construction paper to make a tail instead of using yarn.

Paper Bag Mittens

This is a really great craft to do in the winter, plus it's so cute. If you doing this in a preschool classroom setting, it makes a great bulletin board display when all the children's mittens are are hung up with their names on them.

You'll Need:

- Large Paper Grocery Bag
- A Pencil
- Stapler
- Scissors
- Ribbon
- Tempera Paint
- Paint Brush
- Cotton, Batting, or Newspaper

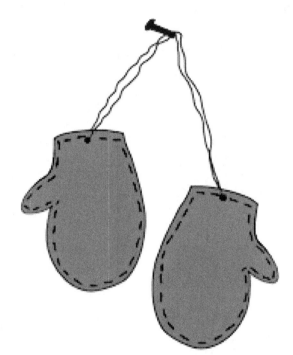

Directions:

1. Trace each of your child's hands onto a flattened out paper bag with their fingers together and their thumb out.

Using this tracing, draw a mitten shape around each hand. Cut out the mitten shapes. When you cut, double the thickness of your paper bag so that you have 2 copies of each mitten, 2 right mittens, and 2 left mittens.

2. Put the 2 right mittens together and staple all around the edge, leaving a gap of about 3 - 4 inches. Make sure the staples are very close together.

3. Stuff cotton, batting, or newspaper inside the hole to stuff your mitten. Once stuffed, staple the opening closed. Do the same thing with the other mitten.

4. Paint your mittens with tempera paint in any color you choose. Let dry completely.

5. Glue or staple a piece of ribbon to each of the mittens at the wrist end to connect the two mittens together.

More Ideas...

- You can add more decorations to your mittens if you want.

- These mittens make great Winter or Christmas decorations.

Craft Tip...

- You can hot glue the mitten together instead of stapling it if you want.

- Hot glue also works well to attach the ribbon connecting the two mittens.

- Remember to keep children away from hot glue so they don't get burned.

Lion Paper Bag Puppet

Kids love to make puppets, and this one is sure to be one of their favorites. It's so simple to make, especially with the help of the template, that little kids should be able to do most of this by themselves.

You'll Need:

- Lion Templates
- Lunch Sized Paper Bag
- Orange Construction Paper
- Yellow Construction Paper
- Scissors
- Glue

Directions:

1. You'll need to print the template that the end of the section onto colored construction paper. The head, jaw, tail, body, and legs should be printed on yellow construction paper. The two mane pieces in the tail tip should be printed on orange construction paper.

2. Cut out all the pieces.

3. Glue the head of the lion onto the mane, making sure to line up on the flat side. Glue the bottom jaw onto the smaller part of the mane, also lining them up on the straight side.

4. Glue the body of the lion onto the paper bag. Make sure you scoot it all the way up to the fold. Glue the legs onto the body. Glue the lower jaw, with the smaller mane already attached, on top of the body and pushed up to the fold.

5. Glue the head, with the mane already attached, onto the part of the back that folds over (actually the bottom of the bag.)

6. Glue the tail onto the back side of the paper bag, opposite of the side with the body attached.

7. Let the glue dry, and then put your hand inside the paper bag to use the puppet.

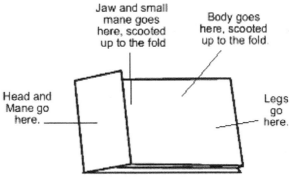

More Ideas...

- Print the template out onto white construction paper and color all the parts. Then proceed through the project.

- Cover the eyes on the template with wiggle eyes.

- Glue some yarn onto the mane to give it a more three dimensional effect.

Craft Tip...

A glue stick works really well for this project because it doesn't wrinkle the paper the way ordinary white glue does.

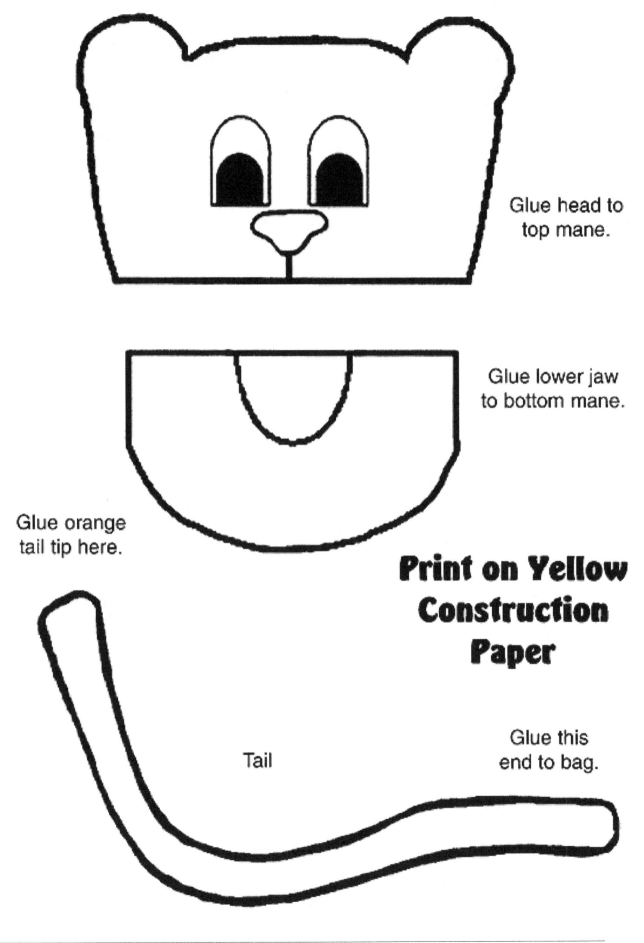

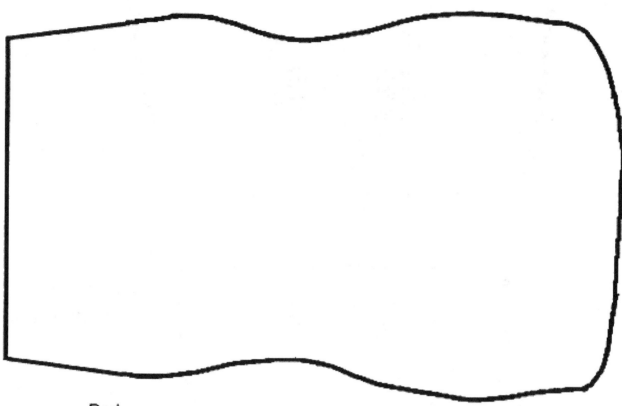

Body

Print on Yellow Construction Paper

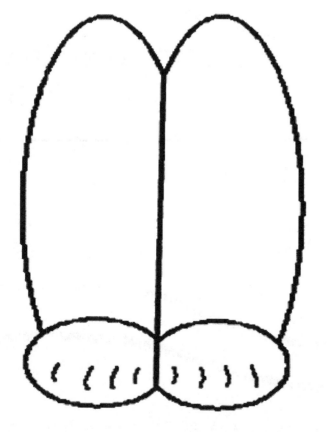

Legs

Print on Orange Construction Paper

Glue head to this part of mane.

148

Exploration and Learning Crafts

Leaf Creatures

This is a great learning activity because it teaches children to try to look at things in a different way... To think out of the box. You may have to get them started, but once they get going, you'll be surprised with what they come up with.

You'll Need:

- Sheet Construction Paper
- Various Leaves
- Crayons or Markers
- Glue

Directions:

1. Go out on a leaf hunting expedition and collect leaves off the ground. Try to get different colors, shapes, etc.

This would be great opportunity to use the fall gathering basket that you made in the paper bag crafts section.

2. Randomly glue a couple of leaves to a piece of paper. Let dry.

3. Using your markers or crayons, try to make those leaves look like people or animals.

NOTE: Be sure to ask questions about each of your child's creatures… Let them explain who or what each one is, their names, etc. This helps children gain ownership over their work.

More Ideas...

- The leaves don't have to be just people or animals, you can make leaves look like cars, planes, buildings, etc.

- You can use other objects like seeds, sticks, etc. to add to your picture.

- Use multiple leaves to create one creature.

- Add other materials to your creatures. For example, wiggle eyes, yarn, feathers, etc. will add a lot to your creatures.

Craft Tip...

- This project works best for the Autumn, when there are plenty of leaves of different shapes, sizes, and colors on the ground.

- Children will enjoy gathering their leaves as much as they enjoy turning them into creatures.

Clay Letters

The something really fun and satisfying about working with clay, and kids absolutely love it. This craft really serves two purposes, to work on identifying letters, and to practice their sculpting ability.

You'll Need:

- 1 Batch Salt Dough Recipe
- Wax Paper
- Elbow Macaroni
- Pencil
- Tempera Paint
- Paint Brush

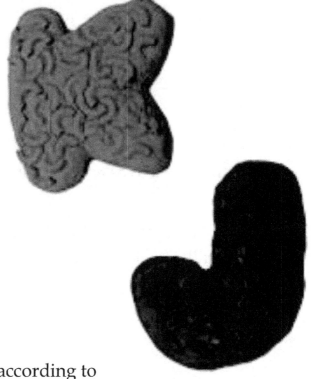

Directions:

1. Prepare a batch of the salt dough according to the directions below.

Salt Dough Recipe

Mix 1 ½ cups of salt and 4 cups of flour in a large bowl. Gradually add about 1 ½ cups of water until the dough forms a ball around the spoon.(If you add too much water, just add a little more flour. If it's too crumbly, add more water.) Pour the dough onto a flat surface and knead it until it is pliable and easily formed.

2. Give the child a piece of wax paper. With a pencil, write out a letter of the alphabet. This will give them a template to follow to make their letter. Show them how to roll the dough and shape it to make the letter on the wax paper.

3. Once the letter is done, press pieces of elbow macaroni into the face of the dough letter. This will create a unique letter design. Let the dough dry out and harden.

The length time it takes to dry depends on the size and thickness of the letter. You can speed up the process by placing the letter on a baking sheet and baking it in a 300° oven for 30 minutes to an hour until hard.

4. After the dough is hardened and cool (if applicable), lay it out on a piece of newspaper and paint it with tempera paint.

More Ideas...

- Do just one letter a week to make this a reinforcement tool for learning the alphabet or in conjunction with a phonics program.

- Create the letters that spell the child's name and put them up on a shelf in the child's room so they see them regularly. It will increase their letter awareness and help them learn to recognize their name, especially since they will admire their creation often.

- Use this idea to create a paper weight to give to Mom or Dad as a Mother's Day or Father's Day gift.

- You can use other types of pasta to press into your clay for a different effect.

- Instead of painting the letters with tempera paint, you could color them with markers.

Name Necklace

This project works particularly well for children who were just learning to write or spell their names. It also works well for helping children to develop their sense of self identity... Plus it doubles as a room decoration!

You'll Need:

- Thin Cardboard
- Construction Paper
- 18 - 24 Inch Piece of Yarn
- Scissors
- Bold Marker
- Hole Punch
- Crayons, Markers, Stickers, etc.

Directions:

1. Cut a piece of thin cardboard that measures 6 x 4 inches. Cut 2 pieces of construction paper that measure 6 x 4 inches.

2. Glue one of the construction paper rectangles onto the front of the cardboard, and glue the other one to the back. Let the glue dry. This will be a name plate.

3. Punch 2 holes in the name plate so that it can be used for a necklace. The holes should be about an inch from each corner on the top of the name plate.

4. With a bold marker, write the child's name across the name plate. Decorate around the name with crayons, markers, stickers, etc.

5. Cut a piece of yarn about 18 - 24 inches long. Tie a large knot in one end. Thread the yarn through one of the holes in the name plate, from the front. The knot should be big enough to keep it from pulling through.

Thread the yarn through the second hole in the name plate from the back and tie a large knot in the end to keep it from pulling though.

More Ideas...

- You can put beads onto the yarn before you thread it through the second hole and tie the knot.

- You can thread pieces of pasta onto the necklace before you thread it through the second hole and tie the knot.

- You can eliminate the need for thin cardboard by using heavy cardstock instead.

- When child isn't wearing their name necklace, they can hang it up in their room at decoration.

- Use this project as a way for the child to practice recognizing their name as well as letters of the alphabet. You can make this name plate with their first name or their entire given name.

Craft Tip...

A glue stick works well for this project instead of white glue.

Print Making

It's amazing to see the look on a child's face the very first time they make a print on their own. In this project, they can help you find the objects to print, create the print board, and make prints, making for a very interesting and hands-on craft.

You'll Need:

- Large Piece of Heavy Cardboard
- Large Paper Plate or Pie Tin
- Paint Roller
- Hot Glue and Gun
- Sheets of Construction Paper
- Various "Printable" Objects

Directions:

1. On a large piece of cardboard, hot glue a variety of objects like leaves, lace, sandpaper, mesh, yarn, etc. Use anything that will make an interesting print.

2. Pour some tempera paint into a large paper plate or pie tin. Roll a paint roller in the paint carefully and roll paint over all the objects on your cardboard. Try to only get paint on the objects and not on the cardboard. You could use a paint brush for this part of the project, but it takes a lot longer to paint the objects.

3. Lay a sheet of construction paper over different objects, or combinations of objects, and lightly rub to get a print of the object.

4. Peel the paper off the cardboard and objects. Let dry completely.

NOTE: If you're working with a very young child, paint may be too messy. You can still do this project however, by showing them how to do rubbings with a crayon or pencil.

More Ideas...

- Try painting different objects different colors.

- See if your child can identify all the objects from the prints. It's a good exercise in spatial thinking and relationships.

- After the paint is dry, try to create pictures out of the prints using markers.

- This is a good group project. Have children help gather print making objects, then have each child do a print of their object to show to the group.

Craft Tip...

Rolling the paint onto the objects is best done by an adult so that paint only gets on the objects and not on the cardboard.

Flower Blow Painting

This is another one of those projects were children get to think outside the box. By doing to blow painting first, letting it dry, and then turning it into something else, they learn to conceptualize things in a different way. Plus it's just a lot of fun!

You'll Need:

- Light Colored Construction Paper
- Tempera Paint
- Water
- A Straw
- Markers
- Scissors

Directions:

1. Thin out tempera paint by adding a few drops of water. It should be thick enough to provide vivid colors and thin enough to drop by drops. Do this with a couple of different colors.

2. Cut a straw in half.

3. Put drops of paint on construction paper. Give the child a piece of straw and have them blow the paint through the straw.

Make sure they understand that they should not put the straw in the paint, just blow the paint with the straw. This will hopefully keep them from sucking up any paint. Don't worry if they do accidentally get paint in their mouth. Tempera paint is mostly made of clay and is non-toxic.

Add more drops and different colors, having child blow each drop of paint. When design is finished, let dry completely.

4. Use markers to draw petals around the paint splatters. Draw on stems and leaves.

Skill Building...

- This is a good craft for helping kids work on their coordination skills and give them practice blowing. If you've ever seen a young child trying to learn how to blow bubbles, then you know that they could use practice developing this skill.

- In addition, they are also getting a lesson in cause and effect. They blow through the straw and the paint drop moves, splatters, spreads out, etc. You can reinforce this concept by asking them to try to move the paint in a certain direction.

Craft Tip...

Don't thin the paint too much. It will appear more like watercolor if you do. In addition to being a much more pastel painting, it will also splatter more when they blow. A little bit thicker paint will splatter a lot less.

Winter Toothbrush Painting

Younger kids will find that this is a really fun way to create a winter painting. By showing them how a toothbrush can be used as a painting tool and lots of different ways, you help them expand their way of looking at things.

You'll Need:

- Black or Dark Blue Construction Paper
- Clean Toothbrush
- White Tempera Paint

Directions:

1. Pour white tempera paint into a small paper plate. Pour some more paint into a second paper plate and thin slightly with water.

2. Dip the toothbrush in the paint and create a winter scene. You may want to suggest something specific to your child, such as: draw a snowman, draw the North Pole, etc.

You may want to demonstrate for the child some of the ways they can use this painting tool. For example:

- You can simply paint with the toothbrush, creating long strokes.
- You can use the toothbrush to make scrubbing strokes.
- You can use the thinner paint to splatter paint over your picture to create snow flakes.

Once your painting is finished, let it dry completely.

Skill Building...

This is a good opportunity for kids to experiment with the different effects they can achieve with a toothbrush. It is a good lesson on creativity and thinking out of the box... Plus it's fun!

More Ideas...

- Sprinkle a little glitter on the painting while the paint is still wet for a pretty, sparkling winter scene.

- Try doing a painting with toothpaste instead of paint. It's bound to get a giggle from your child, and the painting will smell good too!

- Create other toothbrush paintings with other colors on light colored paper and observe the difference with the child.

- Use this technique to create wrapping paper or a background for a card.

Egg Head People

These little egg people are a ton of fun for kids to make. Although when you first do the project, the kids may have a little trouble conceptualizing what it will look like when the grass grows. Once the grass fills in and begins to look like hair, the kids won't be able to stop rubbing their hands across it.

You'll Need:

- An Egg
- Nail or Other Sharp Object
- Potting Soil
- Grass Seed
- Permanent Marker
- Water Colors (optional)
- Regular Markers
- Toilet Paper Tube

Directions:

1. Use a nail to poke a quarter-sized hole in the top of an egg. Pour out the contents and wash out the shell carefully in soapy water. Set aside.

2. Cut a section of a toilet paper tube that's about 2 inches long. This is the egg head body. Decorate the body with markers, drawing on clothes, arms, etc.

3. Put the egg shell on top of the toilet paper tube that you've decorated. Carefully draw on a face. Remove the egg head from the body. Paint the egg shell with water colors, if desired. Let dry.

4. Fill each egg shell about 3/4 full of potting soil. Sprinkle with grass seed. Water lightly and then replace the egg head on the body. Place your Egg Head in a sunny location.

5. Water as often as the grass seed package says it requires and watch as your characters begin to grow "hair." Once the hair grows in, you can cut it, shape it, etc.

> **NOTE:** Raw eggs may contain the salmonella bacteria and pose a serious risk of illness if ingested. Wash shells and keep raw eggs away from children to avoid the risk.

Skill Building...

It's a good lesson for children to plant seeds, tend them, and watch them grow into plants. This is a really fun way to do it!

More Ideas...

- Try doing this with other kinds of seeds. You could make an Egg Head Herb Garden, for example.

- You could also use the "Egg Head" idea to start seedlings for Spring. Start your seeds in the egg shells, and then when they are big enough, you could plant them in your garden... shell and all.

Ink Blot Kites

Kites are great springtime activity. Although I'm not sure if these guys will actually fly, they make great classroom and room decorations.

You'll Need:

- Sheet of Construction Paper
- Tempera Paint
- String or Yarn
- Scissors
- Hole Punch
- 3 Tissues (The kind you blow your nose on)

Directions:

1. Cut a white piece of construction paper into a square. The easiest way to get a square is to fold a corner of the paper to the opposite side, then cut off the excess paper. You now have a diamond with a fold down the center.

2. Lay the diamond back out flat on a table and dribble paint onto one side. Fold the other side of the diamond on top of the paint and smooth down. Open the diamond back up to reveal your ink blot. Let dry.

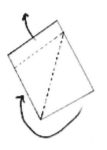 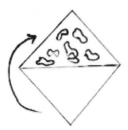 

3. Cut a piece of yarn or string that's about 12 inches long. This will be the kite's tail. Smash the tissue down into a long skinny shape, and tie each of the tissues onto the tail.

You'll have to make the knots gently, so you don't tear the tissue. Try to evenly space the tissues and leave an open spot at the top of the tail so that you can attach it to the kite.

4. Punch a hole in the bottom of the diamond. Attach the kite's tail.

5. Punch a hole in the top of the diamond. Tie a string or piece of yarn to use as a hanger.

Skill Building...

- Children will find the whole idea of ink blots interesting. This is something that they can do entirely by themselves. After they open the paper up, ask them what it looks like to them.

- Most children should be able to tie the tissue pieces to the tail. It's a simple cross, over, pull through tie.

Craft Tip...

- If you have trouble keeping the tissue on the tail, there's a couple of things you can try: tighten down your knots, use a little glue to glue the tissue to the yarn, tie a knot in the yarn directly under the spot where you want each of the tissues to rest

- If you want to decorate the kite's tail, you can use markers, but some tissues actually come in colors other than white.

Holidays

Quick n' Easy Gift Wrap

Wrapping presents is really difficult for children, but with these little gift bags they can feel like they've wrapped their present themselves. This is a really fun and easy project for children of all ages.

You'll Need:

- Small Paper Bag
- Rubber Stamps
- Stamp Pad
- Hole Punch
- Ribbon

Directions:

1. Stamp pictures on a paper bag. Let dry.

2. Put your gift inside. Fold over the top of the bag a couple of inches more or less, depending on the size of the gift inside.

3. Punch 2 holes in the top about 2-3 inches apart and centered on the folded over part. Thread a piece of ribbon or yarn through the one side of the bag to the other. It's up to you to decide which side of the bag is the front and the back.

Tie into a bow, and your bag is sealed shut and ready to present to the gift recipient.

More Ideas...

- Use other materials to tie up your gift such as raffia, yarn, curly ribbon, etc.

- Use crayons or markers to draw pictures on your paper bag instead of stamping.

- Cut out shapes or designs and glue them onto the bag with a glue stick.

- Metallic pens add very nice accents to any gift bag.

- Punch a hole in your gift tag and thread it onto the ribbon before tying up your package.

- Larger gifts may require the use of large grocery store type bags. You can often find these without any store advertising on them.

Craft Tip...

We usually use the kind of rubber stamps that you would use for scrapbooking or card-making, but you could also use kid's stamp markers or self-inking stamps made specifically for kids.

Handprint Key Chains

These little handprint Key chains make terrific gifts for parents and grandparents. They are really easy to make, fun for kids to watch shrink, and make for a great keepsake.

You'll Need:

- Clear Shrink It
- Colored Pencils
- Permanent Marker
- Pencil
- Scissors
- Large Hole Punch
- Brown Paper Bag
- Oven-Proof Tray or Cookie Sheet
- 325° Oven or Toaster Oven

Directions:

1. Preheat oven to 325° (or whatever the manufacturer's directions specify). Trace child's hand on the rough side of the shrink it material with pencil.

2. Color the handprint with colored pencil. Be sure to press hard so that the maximum amount of color transfers onto the shrink it.

3. Cut the handprint out. Punch a hole with a large hole punch on the wrist side of the hand. (If you don't have a larger than standard hole punch, use a standard one and punch a couple of times to make a larger hole.)

4. Write the child's name and the date on the rough side of the handprint with a permanent marker.

5. Cut a piece of brown paper bag to fit inside your tray or cookie sheet. Put handprints, colored side up, on top of paper bag on cookie sheet. Place in preheated oven.

Bake 1 - 3 minutes. Pieces will curl up, shrink, then lay flat again. Take them out of the oven when they have shrunk and are laying flat for about 30 seconds.

6. Once removed from oven, lightly press flat with folded paper or a paper pad. Do not touch until they are cooled… about 15 - 30 seconds.

7. Once cooled completely, put a key ring through the hole to complete the key chain.

More Ideas...

The color can scratch off from the wear and tear of the key chain, but you could simply make one without coloring it. Simply write the name and date of the child before baking with a permanent marker.

These make terrific Mother's Day and Father's Day gifts!

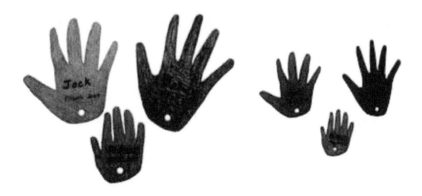

My children's hands before shrinking.   My children's hands after shrinking.

Shrink it material (Commonly under the Shrinky Dinks name) usually shrinks to about 1/3 its original size and becomes 9 times thicker. Once baked, it becomes hard plastic and is very durable.

Hiding In A Pencil Holder

This is a fun little craft that makes a great gift for mom or dad. It's super simple, and all the templates that you need are included.

You'll Need:

- Pencil Holder Template
- 3 Colors Construction Paper
- Empty Can or Container
- Scissors
- Glue
- Pencil
- Markers

Directions:

1. Measure the height of the can you're using and cut a piece of construction paper long enough to cover the container. Wrap it around your container and glue in place.

2. Put the can on a piece of paper and trace around the base with a pencil. Draw in the feet and cut out. Glue the feet onto the bottom of the container.

3. Cut the head, hair, and hands out of construction paper, using the template on the next page. There are three hair styles to choose from.

4. Glue the hair onto the head. Draw on the face with markers.

5. Put glue on the bottom of the head and glue it to the inside front of the can so it looks like he's peeking out. Glue the hands on so they look like he's holding on to the edge of the pencil cup. Glue on the buttons.

More Ideas...

- The best part of this craft is its simplicity, especially for younger children. You can make it more complicated, however, by decorating the outside of the pencil holder.

- Older kids can cut out eyebrows, eyes, and buttons instead of drawing them on with a marker.

- For a more durable pencil holder, try creating this project with craft foam instead of paper.

- This craft would make a great gift for Mom or Dad's office.

Warm Fuzzy

This craft harkens back to my childhood. When I was a kid we would make these little warm fuzzies every Valentine's Day at school and give them to our friends. They're so easy to make that I had to include them here... And they're so cute too!

You'll Need:

- Large Pom Pom
- Construction Paper
- Wiggle Eyes
- Glue

Directions:

1. Cut a heart out of any color construction paper. This will serve as the feet for your warm fuzzy, so make sure the heart is bigger than the diameter of your pom pom.

2. Glue a large pom pom onto the middle of your heart.

3. Glue on 2 wiggle eyes.

More Ideas...

- Give Warm Fuzzies to friends and family as gifts on special holidays... green and red for Christmas, red and pink for Valentine's Day, etc.

- Glue them on cards or gift packages to dress them up.

- Older children can write a tag and glue it between the feet and the pom pom, so that it sticks out. They could name their creatures, write a short poem, or simply say, "I love you!"

- Glue a magnet to the bottom of the feet to make this a refrigerator magnet.

- You can make an army of these at one time so that you can give them to people who just need a Warm Fuzzy!

Skill Building...

- The craft itself provides a good opportunity to reinforce the concept of colors, their names, etc., in addition to giving your child the chance to experiment with putting different color combinations together.

- The real value of this craft is that it provides a doorway for you and your child to explore the idea of good citizenship, kindness, sportsmanship, and generally just "being nice" to others.

    The idea is to give Warm Fuzzies to others when they are "being nice" and for your child to receive Warm Fuzzies when they are "being nice." Even very young children can grasp this concept, and it's never too early to start.

- If you're doing this project in a group setting, like a school or daycare, then you can start a whole new way for the children to relate to each other.

Valentine Dangle Heart

The first time the kids and I made this project, my five-year-old said the hearts were "magic" because they look like they were floating. Only a child could see magic and fishing line... Isn't it great!

You'll Need:

- A Paper Plate
- Red Tempera Paint
- Red Construction Paper
- Fishing Line
- Transparent Tape
- Scissors
- Glue

Directions:

1. Fold a paper plate in half and cut a large half heart. Cut another half heart inside the first to create a heart frame.

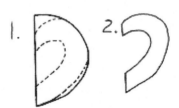

2. Open up the heart and paint it red on what would be the back side of the paper plate. Let dry.

3. Cut 6 hearts the same size out of red construction paper. Hearts should be about 1-2 inches across, depending on the size of your center hole.

4. Cut 3 pieces of fishing line that are about 4-5 inches long. Tape a piece of fishing line to each of the 3 hearts, following along the center.

Glue a second heart over the fishing line to sandwich. Tape the other end of the fishing line to the back side of your heart so that it dangles inside the opening and moves freely.

5. Attach another longer piece of fishing line to the top of the large heart to make a hanger.

Skill Building...

- Ribbon could be used instead of fishing line for a very different look. You may have to punch holes in the plate and tie off ribbon to use this option.

- Make the project more difficult by adding lace, stickers, etc. You can even spray it with glitter for a dazzling effect.

Comments...

This project takes a little bit of help from an adult to complete, but is well worth the effort. Anytime would be happy to present this craft to their sweetheart.

Pot of Gold

This is a fun and simple St. Patrick's Day craft the kids will love. It's also a great project to help illustrate some of the stories that we tell our children on the holiday.

You'll Need:

- Paper Plate
- Yellow and Green Construction Paper
- Black Tempera Paint
- Paint Brush
- White Glue
- Scissors
- Glue Stick
- Gold Glitter

Directions:

1. Cut about a third of the plate off, cutting in a straight line, and discard. Cut an indent in the plate, near the flat spot, on both sides.

2. Paint the back side of the plate black and let dry. This is your pot.

3. Cut out about 10 "coins" from yellow paper. The coins should be about 1-2 inches in diameter.

4. Glue the coins to the unpainted side of the pot so that they stick up above the flat side. When looking from the front, the coins will look like they are sitting in the pot.

5. Cut a shamrock out of green paper and glue to the front of the pot.

6. Squirt glue on the coins and sprinkle with gold glitter. Let dry.

Craft Tip...

Don't just limit yourself to glitter on this project. You could glue sequins, gold beads, or anything else that would make the gold sparkle.

More Ideas...

- You could do this project with a small paper plate, and then glue a construction paper rainbow onto the back of the coins, so that the pot of gold looked like it was at the end of the rainbow.

- Outline the shamrock with glue and sprinkle with green glitter.

- Make a handle for the pot of gold out of a pipe cleaner. Punch holes on both sides of the pot and attach the pipe cleaner.

Pine Cone Easter Bunny

This is a really cute Easter craft they kids can do almost entirely by themselves. The great thing about this project is that when it's done, kids will be really proud to bring it home.

You'll Need:

- 1 1/2 - 2 Inch Pink Pom Pom
- 3 - White Pom Poms (1/2 inch)
- 1 - Small Black Pom Pom (1/4")
- Pink Construction Paper
- 2 - 8mm Wiggle Eyes
- Glue
- Scissors
- Pine Cone (2" or Taller)

Directions:

1. Cut out the ears, front paws, and feet from pink construction paper. Cut two ear centers from white paper.

2. Glue the feet onto the base of the pine cone. Let dry.

3. Glue the cheeks and nose to the large pink pom pom. You may have to hold in place for a few seconds. Glue on eyes.

4. Glue ears onto large pink pom pom. Put glue on the end of each ear and try to work it down into the pom pom a little bit. This will help it hold and stand up straight.

5. Glue the large pink pom pom onto the top of the pine cone. If the tip of the pine cone is too pointy, just break off the point. Again, you may have to hold it for a few seconds.

6. Glue the paws onto the pine cone. Glue the pom pom tail on the back of the pine cone.

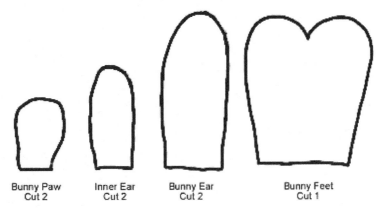

Craft Tip...

If you are working with very small children who will have a hard time gluing on some of the parts on the bunny, you could use hot glue. It cools very quickly and will keep the project moving along.

More Ideas...

The colors suggested for the bunny is only a suggestion. Try making the bunnies all different colors, they'll still be cute.

Handprint Easter Chick

As I've already mentioned in several other projects, I'm crazy about handprint crafts. This little Easter check is really cute and makes for a really fun project during the Easter holiday season.

You'll Need:

- Yellow Construction Paper
- Orange Construction Paper
- Pencil
- Crayons or Markers
- 2 Wiggle Eyes (any size)
- Scissors
- Glue

Directions:

1. Trace both of child's hands onto yellow construction paper. Cut out.

2. Cut out an egg shape that's approximately 5 inches long from yellow construction paper. Cut 2 identical strips of yellow paper that are about an inch wide and several inches long. Cut out an orange triangle to make the chick's beak. Cut out 2 chick feet from orange paper.

3. Decorate the egg shaped piece of paper as if it were an Easter egg with markers or crayons.

4. After decorating the egg, glue the hands to the back of the egg so that they stick out like wings. Also glue on 2 wiggle eyes and triangle beak.

5. Accordion fold the two strips of yellow paper. Glue an orange foot to one end of each of the strips. Glue the other end of each of the strips to the back of the chick to make the legs.

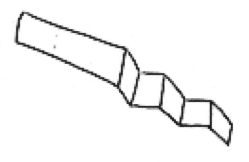

Craft Tip...

An accordion fold is where you fold a strip of paper back and forth the full length of the paper. Each of your folds should be about the same length as the width of your paper, but it definitely does not have to be perfect to turn out well for a project.

More Ideas...

- Glue a few feathers to the top of the head to make a really cute chick.

- Glue a ribbon bow under the beak.

- Don't decorate the egg to make this a non-Easter craft.

Show Your Patriotism

Although this project is done with an American flag, you can easily swap out the basic idea with any flight from any nation. Regardless of which flag you use, this is a great craft for young children.

You'll Need:

- Flag Template
- White Construction Paper
- Red and Blue Crayons or Markers
- Large Craft Stick
- Scissors
- Glue

Directions:

1. Print the template on the next page onto white construction paper.

2. Color the 2 American flags the appropriate colors using markers or crayons. The stripes should alternate red and white, starting with red at the top. The stars should be white (they won't need coloring) and the rectangle behind the stars should be blue.

3. Cut out the 2 American flags, but don't cut on the dotted line that separates them. One easy way to cut them out is to fold them on the dotted line and then cut them out together. This method assures that the two sides will match.

4. Once cut, fold the flags on the dotted line so that the flags are facing out (If you haven't already folded them).

5. Sandwich the large craft stick between the flags and all the up against the fold. Make sure the end of the stick is below the top of the flag. Glue the two sides of the flag together with the craft stick in between them. Let dry completely.

6. Waive your flag and show your patriotism!

NOTE: The national flag of the United States consists of 13 horizontal stripes that are alternately red and white, and the field of blue containing 50 white stars.

The red and white stripes represent the original 13 states.

The 50 white stars represent the present US states.

The United States flag is also called old glory and the Star-Spangled Banner.

Skill Building...

- This is a good opportunity to talk to your child about your country, it's leaders, it's beliefs, etc.

- Talk about what the flag means, symbolically, as well as what each of the colors, stripes, and stars mean.

- Although this project is for an American Flag in celebration of American Independence Day, you can use the same concept to talk about any flag or country.

Show Your Patriotism Template

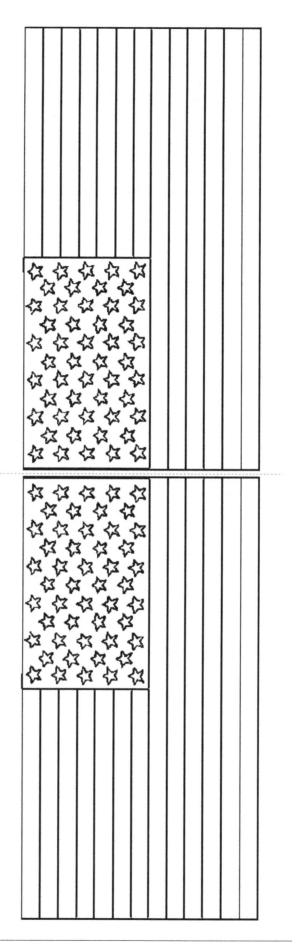

Traditional Candle Centerpiece

This project may look a little bit complicated at first, but it's definitely easy enough for younger children to accomplish on their own, plus it's mostly made out of recycled items. What makes this craft even better, is that it's a really neat project to bring home for just about any holiday, including Christmas Thanksgiving and Easter... It just depends on how you decorate.

You'll Need:

- 3 Toilet Paper Tubes
- White Tempera Paint
- Green Tempera Paint
- Yellow Tissue Paper
- Small Paper Plate
- Red Ribbon
- Scissors
- Glue
- Glitter

Directions:

1. Cut 2 of your tubes to a different height so that you have a full length tube, a medium height tube, and a short tube.

2. Paint each of the tubes with white tempera paint. Sprinkle with glitter while still wet, then let dry completely. Paint the small paper plate green and let dry completely.

3. Group the 3 white tubes together in the center of the paper plate and glue down to the plate. You may want to glue the tubes to each other first to make this a little easier. Let glue dry completely before proceeding to next step.

4. Wrap a red ribbon around all three tubes and tie it in a bow.

5. Cut your tissue paper into 4 inch squares. Put several of the squares over the top of a pencil and insert into the end of each tube. Remove the pencil and you should have "flames" sticking out of your "candles."

More Ideas...

- If you don't want to paint the paper plate green, you could cut out some holly leaves and berries and glue them all around the candles. You could even glue some to the candles.

- This project was really intended for a Christmas centerpiece, but you could change the holiday by simply changing the colors.

Craft Tip...

- Hot glue works really well on this project. It's a lot faster because you don't have to wait for the glue to dry, and it produces a much more sturdy project.

- Remember, hot glue is only for adults. Keep away from children.

Egg Carton Christmas Tree

This is a great way to recycle paper egg cartons and turn them into something beautiful for Christmas. If you're concerned about the possibility of germs on the egg carton, simply microwave the egg carton to kill any possible germs on it.

You'll Need:

- A Paper Egg Carton
- Green Tempera Paint
- Paint Brush
- Brown Pipe Cleaner
- Glue
- Tinsel, Pom Poms, Small Ornaments or Other Things to Decorate

Directions:

1. Cut the end of your egg carton to make a 2 x 2 section of egg cups. Cut 4 more individual egg cups from your egg carton.

2. Set the section of 4 egg cups upside down on a flat surface. (You may have to trim them to get them to fit.) Glue 3 individual egg cups upside down onto the 4 egg cup section. Glue one egg cup on top of the 3 individual egg cups. This will make a pyramid of 4 - 3 - 1. Let the glue dry completely before moving to the next step.

3. Paint the pyramid with green tempera paint. Let dry completely.

4. Cut a brown pipe cleaner into a 5 inch piece. Bend it in half. Insert the ends into the bottom of your tree, piercing the paper. This is your tree trunk.

5. Decorate your tree to make it look like a Christmas tree.

6. Poke the remainder of the brown pipe cleaner completely through the top of the tree and twist the ends together to make a hanger.

More Ideas...

- Sprinkle glitter onto the tree while the paint is still wet.

- Instead of making a plain tree trunk with the brown pipe cleaner, you could thread a small bell and push the pipe cleaner up far enough to hide the bell.

- Use a ribbon to hang your ornament instead of a pipe cleaner.

Craft Tip...

- Hot glue is the best way to go on this project. It's a lot faster because you don't have to wait for the glue to dry, and it produces a much more sturdy project. Besides, the fun part for kids is decorating the tree, not putting it together.

- Remember, hot glue is only for adults. Keep away from children.

Shrinky Dink Ornament

Shrinking links make really great ornaments. There's super durable, easy for kids to make themselves, and look absolutely fantastic when they're done. We makes shrinking dink ornaments just about every year with the kids, that's how much we like them.

You'll Need:

- Ornament Template
- Printer
- Clear Shrink It
- Colored Pencils
- Permanent Marker
- Scissors
- Large Hole Punch
- Brown Paper Bag
- Oven-Proof Tray or Cookie Sheet
- 325° Oven or Toaster Oven
- Ribbon or Yarn for a Hanger

Directions:

1. Preheat oven to 325° (or whatever the manufacturer's directions specify). Trace the template on the next page onto the rough side of your shrink it material.

2. Color the ornament with colored pencils. Be sure to press hard so that the maximum amount of color transfers onto the shrink it.

3. Cut the template out. Punch a hole in the template where indicated. (You can use a standard hole punch for this project, but the hole will be pretty small and more difficult for a child to thread through a hanger.)

4. Write the child's name and the date on the rough side of the ornament with a permanent marker.

5. Cut a piece of brown paper bag to fit inside your tray or cookie sheet. Put handprints, colored side up, on top of paper bag on cookie sheet. Place in preheated oven. Bake 1 - 3 minutes (read the directions on the shrinky dink package). Pieces will curl up, shrink, then lay flat again. Take them out of the oven when they have shrunken and are laying flat for about 30 seconds.

6. Once removed from oven, lightly press flat with folded paper or a paper pad. Do not touch until they are cooled, about 15 - 30 seconds.

7. Once cooled completely, put a piece of ribbon or yarn through the hole and tie together to make a hanger.

Craft Tip...

- Shrink it material usually shrinks to about 1/3 it's original size and becomes 9 times thicker. Once baked, it becomes hard plastic and is very durable.

- Depending on your printer, you may be able to actually print the template directly onto the shrink it material. Check the directions on your shrink it package for printer requirements.

More Ideas...

- Embroidery floss makes a nice and easy hanger.
- I did one of these in Brownies when I was 6 and I still hang it on my Christmas tree with fondness every year.

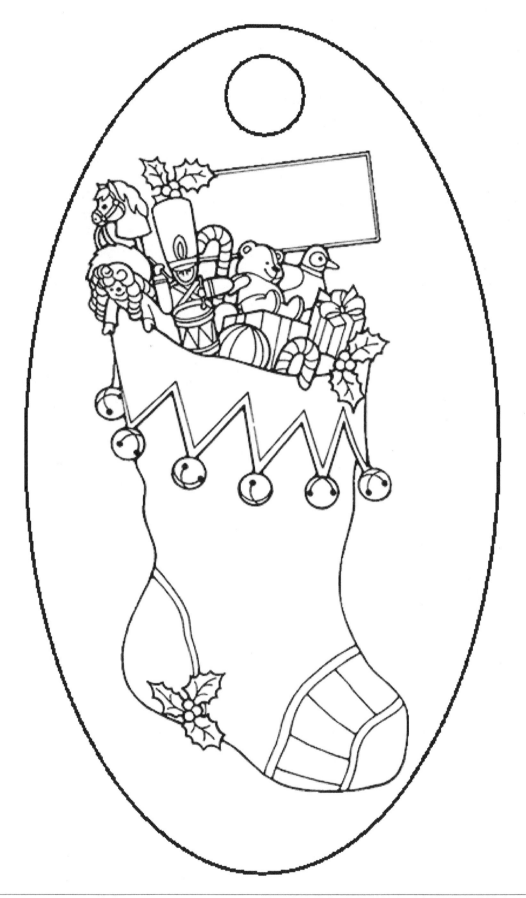

Toilet Paper Tube Turkey

This project is a great way to get away from the standard pinecone Turkey or handprint Turkey. It's super easy to make and even comes with the template!

You'll Need:

- Turkey Template
- Printer and Paper
- Toilet Paper Tube
- Crayons
- Scissors
- Glue

Directions:

1. Print the template at the end of this section onto white printer paper or white construction paper. Color the pieces and cut them out. Don't forget to put a beak, eyes, and a waddle on your turkey's head.

2. Cut a toilet paper tube into a section that is about 2 inches long. Cover with brown piece of construction paper measuring 6 x 2 inches. Glue in place.

3. Glue the turkey's body parts onto the tube according to the diagram below. The body will go on the front of the tube. The tail feathers will go on the back of the tube, opposite of the body. Glue his feet onto the bottom of the tube.

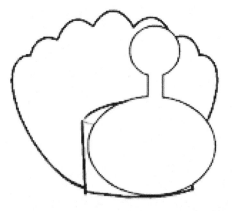

More Ideas...

- Glue wiggle eyes onto the face over the ones drawn on the template.

- You can make this project more challenging for older kids: Print the template out on brown construction paper. Cut individual turkey feathers of different colors of construction paper and glue them over the feather template. Cut out pieces of construction paper to make the beak, waddle, feet, etc. instead of coloring them.

- Make these turkeys Thanksgiving Dinner place holders by writing the name of each person on the body of the turkey and placing them on the table in front of each place.

Craft Tip...

Glue sticks work really well for this project. They dry quickly and are a lot less messy.

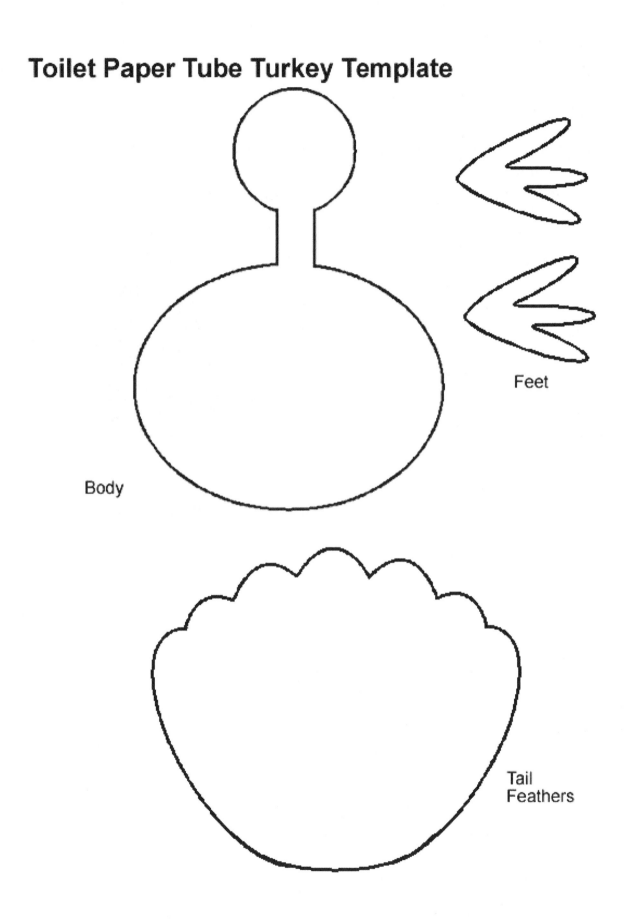

Paper Plate Witch

This is a really fun project for kids to do for Halloween. In fact it's so easy to do, that little kids can do the entire thing on their own. It's also nice because you can make it is scary or as funny as you choose.

You'll Need:

- 9 Inch Paper Plate
- Green Tempera Paint
- Paint Brush
- Markers
- Scissors
- Black Construction Paper
- Yarn Pieces
- Plastic Spiders

Directions:

1. Paint the back side of a paper plate with green tempera paint. Let dry.

2. Draw a witches face onto the plate with a markers. You can make the witch look scary or silly. Glue pieces of yarn all around the top edge of the plate to make hair.

3. Cut a large black equilateral triangle measuring about 6 inches long on each side. Cut a large black oval that measures about 10 - 11 inches long and 3 - 4 inches wide. Glue the triangle onto the middle of the oval so that it looks like a flat witch's hat.

4. Glue or staple the hat onto the witch's head. The hat should not conform to the shape of the plate, it should just be glued onto the flat part of the plate and be loose at the edge of the plate.

Make sure that the hat overlaps some of the hair so that it looks like the hat is sitting on the witches head.

5. Glue plastic spiders onto your witch. You may have to use hot glue to make them stick.

More Ideas...

- Use large wiggle eyes to make a silly looking witch.

- Cut out pieces of construction paper for the eyes, nose, warts, mouth, etc. to make this a more challenging project.

- Bright neon colored yarn works well for this witch, especially if you want to make one that is more silly than scary.

- You could use raffia, construction paper, straw, or other materials for the hair.

Craft Tip...

Using a stapler to put the hat on will help it hold better and be quicker than glue. Kids won't notice the staples, so it doesn't detract from the craft.

Q-Tip Skeleton

I absolutely love this little skeleton craft because I think it's so cute. This project is great to use for Halloween, but you can also use it for a theme project for the letter X, as in x-ray.

You'll Need:

- Sheet Black Construction Paper
- Small Piece of White Paper
- Black Marker
- Chalk
- Q-Tips
- Glue

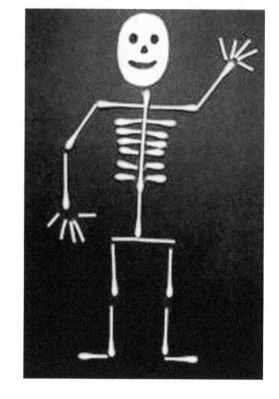

Directions:

1. Cut an oval out of white construction paper and put a face on it with a black marker. This will be the head of your skeleton. Glue it onto the black piece of construction paper near the top of the page.

2. Draw an outline of a skeleton in chalk underneath the skeleton's head. Don't make the outline one continuous line of the paper. Actually draw lines where each of the "bones" is supposed to go so it doesn't confuse the child.

3. Pour a small amount of glue into a small paper plate. Break up several Q-tips into different sizes for the child if they are younger, or show older children how to break them into the sizes they want. These with be the "bones" of your skeleton.

4. Choose a bone, dip it into the glue, and place it on the outline of your skeleton.

More Ideas...

- This is a fun idea to do for Halloween, but you could also use it for a lot of other themes such as: the human body, letter x (x-ray), etc.

- If you're doing this project for Halloween, you could draw a scary picture on your paper first with chalk and then glue your skeleton in after.

- If you are pretty talented, you could build your Halloween scene out of Q-tips too.

- You could use some other material to make your skeleton, like toothpicks, for example.

Craft Tip...

Younger children may have a little trouble with the idea of dipping their "bones" into the glue and make a real mess. You could, however, put the glue directly on the paper and help them avoid some of the mess.

Clothespin Bat

This is a fun and simple project for kids to do for Halloween, but you can also use this craft in conjunction with other themes such as animal themes nocturnal themes or even jungle themes. You could even make this batch as an example of something black if you're trying to teach children colors.

You'll Need:

- Bat Template
- Black Construction Paper
- Printer
- Scissors
- Pinch-Type Clothespin
- Glue
- 2 - 7mm Wiggle Eyes

Directions:

1. Print out the bat template directly onto black construction paper, or copy it onto black paper. Cut out the pieces.

2. The end of the clothespin that you hold to pinch it open is the top of the bat. Glue the bat's body onto the clothespin. The bat's body should cover the entire length of the clothespin.

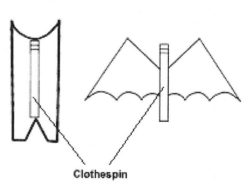

Glue the bat's wings to the opposite side of the clothespin in the center. It really doesn't matter if you put the body or the wings on first, as long as they are on opposite sides of the clothespin.

3. Glue the wiggle eyes onto the bat.

More Ideas...

- This project is really cute when done with craft foam instead of construction paper.

- This is a great project to use in decorating for Halloween. You can clip your bats to curtains, furniture, tableclothes, other decorations, etc.

- Instead of wiggle eyes, use a hole punch to make a couple of circles of white paper, glue them onto your bat, and put a black pupil in the center.

- To make scary bats, use red construction paper eyes.

Craft Tip...

This is a good project to use hot glue on. It sticks well to the clothespin and is more sturdy. This is an adult job, however, and should be kept away from children.

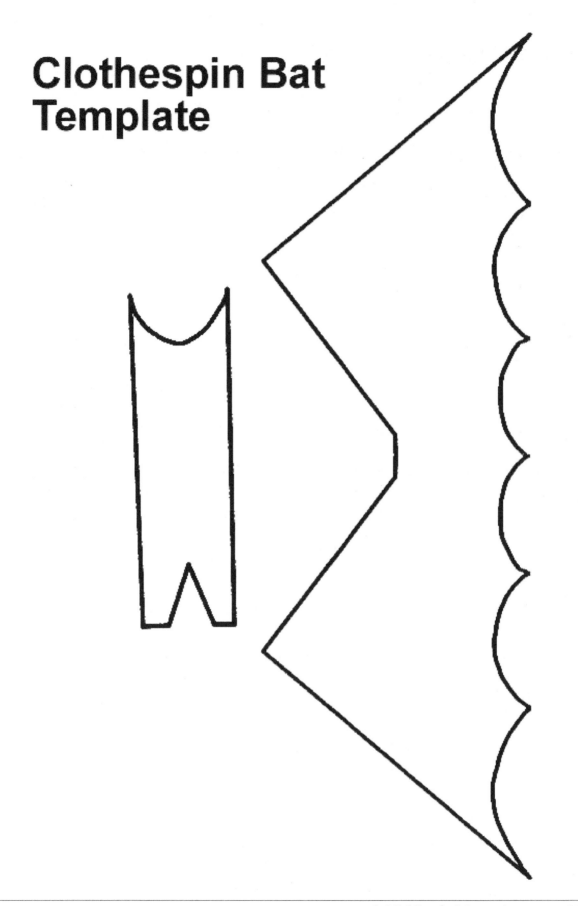

Christmas Scape

This is a fun project the kids will enjoy putting together, but it's also something that they will really enjoy playing with. In fact, you might find even older kids playing with this one.

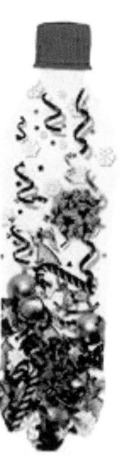

You'll Need:

- Clean Soda Bottle with Lid
- Hot Glue
- Glitter
- Water
- Various Small Christmas Objects and Ornaments

Directions:

1. Put miniature ornaments, glitter, tinsel, plastic snow, etc. into a clean, clear plastic soda bottle. Anything that fits a Christmas theme and is small enough to fit through the neck of the bottle can go in.

2. Fill the bottle up to the neck with water.

3. Put hot glue into the lid and screw the lid onto the bottle while the glue is still hot. This will seal the bottle.

4. Turn the bottle upside down and watch as all the objects float to the other end, then turn it right side up.

NOTE: This is a fascinating project for younger kids, but don't forget the glitter. It's just not the same without it.

More Ideas...

- You can make a "scape" for just about any holiday or theme, provided you can find objects small enough to fit through the neck of the bottle.

- Add food coloring to the water in your Christmas Scape to create a very different effect.

- Try creating "scapes" from different types of containers. Containers with wider mouths will make it a little easier to find objects that fit.

Craft Tip...

- You can find a lot of small objects and tiny ornaments at a dollar store or novelty store.

- Things that are plastic work best and can range from party favors to cake decorations.

Coming Soon...

Little Kid Best Loved Book Activities
Crafts, Recipes, and Learning Activities Based on 50 Popular and Award Winning Children's Books

****

Little Kid Christmas Crafts

****

Crafty Concoctions for Little Kids
Recipes and Instructions for Times of Homemade Art and Craft Supplies and How To Use Them

****

Little Kid Seuss Theme Activities
Crafts, Recipes, and Learning Activities Based on The Most Popular and Loved Dr. Seuss Books

****

Little Kid Halloween Crafts

****

Little Kid Edible Art
Recipes That Kids Love to Make, Eat, and Create With

Made in the USA
Middletown, DE
07 August 2019